Access:

Technology and access to communications media

B.R. Webster

Unesco

ISBN 92-3-101271-1
French edition 92-3-201271-5

Published by The Unesco Press
7, Place de Fontenoy, 75700 Paris (France)

Printed in the workshops of Unesco

Preface

In recent years, a good deal of attention has been focused on public access to the communication media, on participation in media organization and production, and on the potential of media for education, especially life-long education, at the level of the local community. For this reason, under its Regular Programme for 1973-1974, Unesco began a series of studies of community media, with the general theme of "Access". A number of facets have been involved in the inquiry. There is firstly the question of participation by the public in the management of media systems, and in programme production itself. Secondly, there is the question of access to media materials - the range of choice available, and the possibility of feedback and dialogue between producers and audiences. Thirdly, there is the perspective of life-long education, and the contribution which communication media may make to such a process. To what extent can modern technologies allow for "self-service" approaches to education, offering a personalized course of study, an individual research programme, or merely the opportunity to browse?

A number of these surveys are nearing completion, and will be published independently, but one of the fundamental constraints is that of technology itself. To what degree does technology assist in this programme of access, and to what extent does it inhibit progress. How rapidly is the situation changing, and what further changes may be anticipated in the foreseeable future?

The purpose of the present report is to discuss such questions from a technological perspective. Its author bridges the two worlds of education and technology; he is Head of the School of Electrical Engineering, Plymouth Polytechnic, United Kingdom, and Director of the Devon Educational Television Service. He is therefore well qualified to evaluate current options, to monitor progress and to sift probability from possibility. Without this foundation, it is clear that much of the present debate and experimental activity exists in a vacuum, and the risk of duplicata, or of pursuing dead ends, could be considerable.

Contents

The author, B. R. Webster, born in 1926 in the United Kingdom, bridges the two worlds of education and technology. He is Head of the Department of Electrical and Electronic Engineering, Plymouth Polytechnic, United Kingdom, and Director of the City of Plymouth Educational Television Service. He is the author of numerous articles and reports appearing in professional and technical journals. He is a Fellow of the Institution of Electrical Engineers, the Institution of Electronic and Radio Engineers, a member of the Royal Television Society, the International Broadcasting Institute, and a founder member of the National Educational Closed Circuit Television Association and former Chairman of its national technical committee. In addition, upon its formation in 1967, he was appointed by the Secretary of State for Education to membership of the National Council of Educational Technology.

Author's acknowledgements

Colleagues in the library and in my own and other schools of Plymouth Polytechnic have been very helpful at all times in guiding me to sources of information and in checking my endeavours to explain their complex worlds in simple terms.

It is to Miss Janet Morris of the United Kingdom's Council for Educational Technology that I owe the warmest thanks. She willingly undertook a heavy burden of background research and then raised the critical questions which helped to crystallize ideas. Without her intellectual stimulation, constant encouragement and assistance this book would not have been finished before the end of the decade it attempts to preview.

Bernard R. Webster

Introduction

From the days when all knowledge, information and skills were transferred by word of mouth, evolution of the processes of transfer can be represented by a step function. The points of change coincide with the introduction of static recording - writing, reproduction of static recording - printing, dynamic recording for reproduction - the new media. Throughout the twentieth century the change to the new media has continued and this transition period will end only when the media are fully accepted as a normal occurrence in all spheres of human activity. The plateau which will be reached can probably only be superceded by, for example, information transfer by direct electrical injection into the brain (see figure 1).

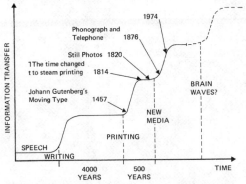

Fig. 1 –The Development of Information Transfer

Thousands of years elapsed between the introduction of writing and the advent of printing. A quiescent period of several hundred years since the introduction of printing has now given way to a transition period, which although extending through several generations, appears on the total time scale of man's history as a period of very rapid change.

The purpose of this study is to survey this transition period and to anticipate some of the problems likely to be encountered before it is complete. As in any transitional process, established practices are being rethought and redesigned, and in the initial stages this often leads to anomalies and mistakes being made along the way. Technological solutions acceptable in one place may prove economically unacceptable in another and vice versa. Money has been invested in new devices which have rapidly foundered through failure to meet market demand, or an underrating of the time and money required for associated developments essential to their acceptance.

Moreover, although the study is principally concerned with technology, the forms and potential of technology cannot be considered apart from their environment. Particularly when we try to separate out probability, over a measured time span, from possibility, we have to consider such factors as public and commercial demand, cost effectiveness, production techniques, the development and sophistification of supporting infrastructures and political and economic circumstances, since it is these, quite as much as technical capacity, which will shape the future.

The report therefore begins with a consideration of the types of access, at individual, group and community levels, and of the prerequisites and limitations affecting their development. These will determine, not only overall progress, but also local variations (for example, as between the developed and the developing world). It then considers the means which permit, or encourage, public access, including not simply technical forms and processes, but also the principles of systems theory on which so much recent work depends, in social and management as well as engineering fields.

With this background, specific technological developments are discussed, across a variety of communication forms. These are finally related to likely trends over the next decade, taking into account their circumstances of growth.

Types of access

Access to the media can be categorized in several ways. First there is a numbers spectrum extending from the individual through small and large groups up to whole nations or even supra-national language groups.

Secondly, there is a spectrum of the degree of activity involved in the process of gaining access. This ranges from the completely passive through various stages of feedback and interaction to the truly participatory processes of access.

Thirdly, access may be considered in terms of its purpose or function, which may be anything from an individual wishing to learn to a government wishing to control a populace.

A. INDIVIDUAL, GROUP, COMMUNITY AND UNIVERSAL ACCESS

Although in one sense every individual is at all times a member of several groups - racial, language, community, etc. - in another sense he may be thought of as a completely independent human being, and the type of access to communication which he has will depend on whether he is alone or part of a particular group at the time. The individual in his home, the student in some form of study carrel or the senior citizen browsing in the public library may all have a personal and particular relationship with the media they are using. Each will have his own particular reason for desiring access, whether this be for pleasure, information or serious study. For every situation and purpose there will be an optimum interface between the individual and the medium, which will determine such parameters as type-face, sound level, picture size, picture brightness.

When the individual joins a group his own requirements do not change but the presentation of the media may need to in order to produce the same result. For example, the individual requires a picture frame size which defines a certain solid angle in space, but this may be achieved by a small screen close to the individual viewer or by a large screen at a much greater distance from a large group.

When an individual seeks feedback or participatory access to the mass media this may be possible in only very limited ways. While an individual may write to a newspaper, or phone-in to broadcast programmes, he cannot produce a television programme without joining a group of like-minded people. Technological developments will not change this situation, but they could make possible, through the development of home terminals, the connexion of the individual in a more active sense than is possible at present, to a wide variety of sources of entertainment, instruction and information. Simple feedback arrangements could also present the individual with the opportunity, for example, to participate in a referendum, select groceries, choose a course of study answer a multi-choice question paper or dial for one of a large number of entertainment channels.

A small group such as a study circle or class in an educational or training institution may wish to participate in collective listening or viewing. With a simple receiving set the form of the group's access is very largely predetermined. Any tutorial comments must either precede or follow the group activity and discussion must follow it. However, with the addition of a cassette recorder tutorial comment and discussion can be interspersed between segments of the programme.

Community access in terms of the broadcast media is directly related to the area and total population served, the degree of involvement felt by any community within this area will be inversely proportional to the size of the total population. The growing demands from communities, particularly within urban areas, to be allowed access to the broadcast media has in many places changed from political action to a more direct approach, made possible by a developing technology which has led to cheaper, light-weight equipment which can be operated by relatively untrained personnel.

Paradoxically, universal access to broadcast programmes could become a reality sooner in some developing countries than in those parts of Europe and North America where a large proportion of the population already have the opportunity to receive television as well as radio. In a country having the chance to install a national broadcasting system for the first time, satellites or modern cable networks could bring more channels to all the people more quickly than will be economically possible in a country which already has a massive capital investment in earlier forms of broadcasting.

B.   PASSIVE, INTERACTIVE AND ACTIVE ACCESS

The passive end of the activity spectrum is in the unconscious or subliminal reception of advertisers' messages. The individual who goes to a library to select a book, to a news-agent to select a journal, or merely pushes a button on his television receiver to choose a channel is beginning to be active in his relationship with the media.

The simplest type of interaction is possibly the use of a request card, whether for a library book or for a tune to be played on the radio. If each member of an otherwise passive audience is provided with a single push-button to enable him to record a vote in response to any question, it is easy to discover the percentage of the audience which holds any particular view or opinion. This technique has been used successfully in a number of broadcast programmes and could be extended to cover a complete community if the facility was included in its cable network. The provision of five push-buttons instead of one permits the system to be used for higher levels of interaction; in particular prestructured learning programmes can be pursued and assessments based on multi-choice questions can be made.

Higher degrees of interaction become possible when a return path with the capability of carrying speech is provided. Modern equipment allows a number of listeners or viewers to be connected directly via the normal telephone system to the studio from which a live radio or television programme is being broadcast.

However, the need to prebook the connexion and the limitations imposed by the duration of the programme mean that only a very small percentage of those who wish to can actually participate in the live programme; the percentage will be much larger in a closed circuit system, e.g. on a college campus where lectures are distributed via television to a viewing room equipped with talkback facilities.

Participatory access can occur in two ways, the first is by a political decision or an organizational arrangement which allows a group to use established production facilities inevitably assisted by the normal staff who operate and maintain them, the second is by a group setting up its own production facilities, with its members learning how to operate and maintain equipment. In the former case the transmission of the finished programme to some known audience will be automatically ensured, but in the latter, the group will have to seek out a means of distributing its product to any potential audience and will have to face the problems which this brings.

C.   PURPOSES AND FUNCTIONS OF ACCESS TO THE MEDIA

Traditional modes of access to the media are at present undergoing considerable change. Some of the changes have incurred because of altered social conditions and pressures; some have been produced by new technical developments, such as cable networks.

Traditionally, especially in the mass media, access has been considered in terms of freedom of choice. Television viewers, newspaper readers, have demanded and have been offered a selection of materials and formats. It has rarely been a hotly debated point that the choice is largely negative: the right to reject unwanted material, rather than to specific exact requirements. This has been the case whether the character of the material - whether it is in entertainment; in information, from various news services; or for instruction, in educational broadcasting and audio-visual media.

Naturally, the producers of the media have been at some pains to consult their audiences, through opinion polls, surveys and the like, and in the case of instructional materials, these have often been carefully preplanned and piloted. But the notion of direct participation by audiences has not been a major issue.

The situation naturally differs from place to place. In a state where the media are directly controlled by government, government representatives may have the only means of access to media productions, in many cases using them for the transmission of information to the people, keeping firm control on all the programmes transmitted. The situation may be completely different in a country where the media are commerically or privately sponsored, or where a public corporation, under independent management, has been created.

In many cases, the range of access is increased

for special purposes, including those directly associated with government. Provision is usually made for public service or emergency announcements, usually by statutory or contractual agreement. Democratic access to broadcast time and facilities may also mean that opposing political parties are allocated agreed amounts of air-time, especially during election periods, the amount allowed being calculated according to some proportional formula.

This situation has at times been further relaxed to allow an individual or organization the opportunity to reply when rights have been infringed. And in education, in particular, access is given in many ways, with time allowed for educational programmes produced by a variety of agencies to be screened on national television, or broadcast over national radio networks.

However, in the last few years, the demands for access have crystallized more than ever before, as people have become more socially aware and conscious. People have not only required the right to information, but the right to answer back to the media, to select and help in shaping its productions, to participate in the production process. This new consciousness expresses itself in a variety of ways, most of which make demands upon technology. At the national level, organized groups and individuals are being allowed time and facilities on major broadcast networks; separate public channels are being added to cable networks (where channel capacity is greater); many programmes, such as "phone-in" programmes, depend primarily upon audience participation and involvement. The new, cheap and portable ranges of audio and video equipment are being used by private groups to articulate their own viewpoints, sometimes directly to a local community, sometimes through existing distribution channels. The scope of this activity is considerable and is being considered extensively in other Unesco studies, in the series of which this is a part, but the kind of demand for public participation from which they spring is lucidly illustrated in the following extract:

... "although it is still scarcely more than a faint shift in the wind, the growing enthusiasm for access and participation in all areas of life is putting pressure on the broadcasting institutions to place the means of communication in the hands of those who feel they have something to say instead of reserving them for those who are professionally trained or officially invited to broadcast: in short, to break down the barrier between the élite who transmit and the mass who listen and view". [1]

D. THE ACCESS MATRIX

Simultaneous consideration of the three aspects of access described in this chapter may be facilitated by use of the three-dimensional matrix below (figure 2). In this the two continuous spectra of numbers of participants and degree of interaction have each been divided into four convenient bands, but as previously discussed these merge and overlap so that more than one mode of access may be apparent in a single operation.

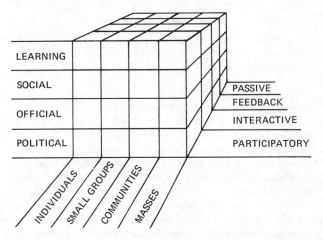

Fig. 2 – The Access Matrix

Many of the above elements are already commonplace; for example, learning - passive - masses would describe educational radio broadcasting. Others are found only in certain countries; for example, political - interactive - individual could describe a phone-in response to a party political television broadcast. Still others exist only in very limited areas; thus social - participatory - community could describe video programmes being made by community action groups in North America for transmission over cable networks.

The matrix also enables us to identify examples of access which are not yet available. So political - feedback - masses might describe the use of a domestic television cable network, with push-buttons allowing voting in national referenda.

(1) "The future of broadcasting" - a report to the Social Morality Council. Eyre Methuen. London 1974.

CHAPTER 2

Prerequisites and limitations on access

In any developed country where the mass media are accepted as part of everyday life it is not until there is some disruption in services that the normal ease of access is appreciated. A television programme at the turn of the knob, a morning newspaper pushed through the door, a seat reservation at the push of a button - all are everyday occurrences. Yet in all these cases there are limitations, sometimes deliberately imposed for political or commercial reasons, but often hidden or unobstrusive, which affect access, and certainly for most of the world's population there are many limitations on access to every type of media. Not all of these limitations are technical. Some derive from the individual (such as his language, his existing skills, education, knowledge and motivation). Others derive from the media themselves (such as cost, technical complexity, reliability, user skills). Still others stem from an interaction of forces within the environment in which the user/receiver lives, works or studies, and in which the media have to operate.

It is not the function of this report to give extensive consideration to social or economic factors. But they cannot be ignored, as they may all have technological implications (a limitation of language, for example, may be solved by providing for multiple audio tracks, in several languages). It is therefore necessary, before considering means, to identify the main limits upon, and prerequisites for, development, in order to understand the potential of technology and to forecast ahead. The areas considered here, briefly, are stylistic (linguistic, socio-linguistic and socio-cultural), technical, operational, political, freedom of choice and environmental.

Before access in any real sense of the word can be achieved, it is important that these limitations are recognized and if possible eliminated.

A. STYLISTIC LIMITATIONS

1. Linguistic

Discounting the relatively few people in the world who are multilingual the first essential for anyone wishing to profit from or enjoy any offering of the media is that it should be in his own language. In the case of film or television, dubbing or subtitling may not provide a completely acceptable substitute, although the provision of alternative audio tracks may be quite acceptable for any programmes in which the "talking-head" plays little part. On a regional basis, local accents cannot easily be transferred to another situation; locally produced material is usually the most suitable.

2. Socio-linguistic

All types of media are directed at a specific audience. Each newspaper printed is aimed at a certain class of reader and not only its content but also its style of writing and presentation are geared to suit the tastes of its target audience. The language used in a popular tabloid paper, a television talk show or a soap opera will be intentionally scaled down to match the intellectual level of the reader/viewer, whereas quality newspapers and documentaries will aim higher. There is little evidence to show that consumers change their habits unless their own circumstances and environments change.

These socio-linguistic factors have implications for developing countries which hope to use the mass media as a means of reaching the majority of the population to pass on information on agriculture, hygiene, birth control, etc. The material must be at the correct level of sophistication before it is acceptable.

3. Socio-cultural

Socio-cultural limitations are immediately apparent in most proposals for exchange of programmes - at regional, national and international levels. Material produced in a developed country is rarely suitable for distribution to audiences in the developing nations. To take a simple example based solely on content, basic reading programmes developed for children in the United States often contain references to household terms such as "refrigerator" and "bathroom", yet to a child in an Indian village these words would mean nothing.

Each locality in a developing country has its own folk history and culture which are now often used as a vehicle for a deeper social or educational message. Conversely, care has to be taken to ensure that material, if produced by an outside team, does not disregard or in any way offend the deeply held beliefs of the audience. These considerations are equally applicable to developed countries, where religion can divide a country, or attitudes towards authority be different between sects or generations. Any material which does not take into account the cultural developments of the audience cannot hope to transfer information successfully.

4. Professionalism

Professionalism can be a limitation on access to press, radio and television in two ways. First the high standards in both production and technical quality which professional broadcasters have attained tend to set a standard which educational and community users with less money, staff and equipment cannot hope to equal. There is therefore a bias against their products which may be difficult to redress by other qualities, particularly the content, of the productions.

Secondly, because much broadcasting is entertainment orientated, production styles have been established which are often quite inappropriate for other purposes. For example, viewers of broadcast television are conditioned to expect some picture on their screens throughout the normal transmitting schedule, but for educational purposes a blank screen or static caption may be desirable for several minutes while the viewers undertake some exercise prescribed by the programme. The imprint of professionalism is to be found to some degree on every viewer who expects the technicalities and grammar of the television which he watches to conform fairly closely to the professional norms set by experienced broadcasters. This has considerable influence on those who wish to produce "community television" - i.e. "television by the people, for the people, about the people". Although the

equipment they use may present no technical problems they need some "assistance" or "training" from television professionals before the programmes they produce are acceptable to a mass audience. However well-intentioned the professional may be in offering his "assistance", it is still likely to be seen as a form of "interference", and in any case will have some effect on the material produced.

The standards of national broadcasting networks may be too high, too costly and unnecessary for many purposes. One of the criticisms which has been levelled at the trained professional is that when transported to a different situation (e.g. an educational institution or a developing country) he finds it difficult to reorientate himself and admit that his high professional standards and expectations may not be suitable or relevant to his new situation.

B. TECHNICAL LIMITATIONS

Technical limitations on the use of equipment which provides access to the media are being steadily eroded by new developments. The following examples illustrate this process.

1. Power requirements

Early radio receivers using valves, even if they could have been produced in sufficient quantities, would have been quite unsuitable for providing large numbers of people in the country areas of Africa or India with access to radio broadcasts, primarily because the power requirements of the set would have demanded a mains supply of electricity or very large batteries. Transistors require far less power than valves and thus have made possible the production of receivers which need only a very small and easily portable battery to drive them.

2. Weight requirements

Early video tape recorders were very large, heavy machines. Other considerations apart, the achievement of minimal weight requirements to make a video recorder suitable for use by an individual, in any location he might choose, has only recently been made possible by developments in electronics technology.

3. Operational simplicity requirement

Throughout the early years of television every television camera had not only a camerman to point it in the right direction but also a highly qualified engineer operating the camera control unit to produce an acceptable picture. The operational simplicity requirement of the unskilled or semi-skilled groups who wish to use television cameras has already been met by those electronic developments which have produced fully automatic camera control units.

4. Reliability requirement

The reliability requirement is very high for all types of equipment intended for use in any environment which is potentially hostile to it, either by reason of climatic conditions or handling by unskilled users. Much expensive equipment has gone out of service and rotted away after a minor fault has occurred early in its life. This state of affairs is often blamed on the inadequacy of maintenance arrangements and the problem of correcting the original design is overlooked. The development of manned space craft gave a tremendous fillip to reliability engineering which is based on a study of the causes of failure originating in production processes and inadequate testing methods. Such new techniques combined with solid state electronics could lead to highly reliable products which, although vitally needed in many situations, are often not made available by manufacturers for commercial reasons.

5. Educational requirements

Specific educational requirements for equipment to be used in schools, including increased attention to such items as safety, robustness and reliability are often not met because the extra costs are prohibitive. Educational users are increasingly forced to buy the cheaper mass produced items designed for the domestic market.

C. USER SKILLS

1. Operation

Mass media communicate their message adequately only when they are technically well received and are being used intelligently by their audience. The user has to know how to operate the television or radio set, how to switch it on, tune it and make simple adjustments before an acceptable signal is obtained. The training given will depend on the situation in which the media are to be used. For example, in a developing country it may be that one or two people in a village are made responsible for the equipment, which is almost always a novelty to the audience. In a developed country, however, say in the classroom, all teaching staff usually need to operate media hardware at some time and therefore every teacher should be made to feel confident that he can handle the equipment in his class.

In any technologically developed society, classroom experience must be seen by the child as being relevant to the outside world. His teacher has to look and feel at home with these modern techniques with which the child is often more familiar.

2. Use

Within the educational context specific training in use of equipment by pre- or in-service courses must be given to all teachers if the hardware is to be used to the best effect. The overhead projector is a good example, since, although the equipment itself is simple to operate, provided care is taken over positioning, it is essential to give the user information on the various types of associated software.

Provided that television programmes are of a suitable nature for their intended audience some support material is usually required if the medium is to be put to the best use. The teacher has to be trained to integrate television in the classroom into the pupils' total environment, rather than, as sometimes happens, regarding television as a separate entity needing no effort on his part. Numerous examples are cited of equipment gathering dust in cupboards once the enthusiast who ordered them has left the school and his colleagues have not received the appropriate training in their use. It is therefore essential that all teachers and not just a favoured few, are given an early opportunity to be trained.

It has already been indicated that some degree of training is essential for production of material. Anyone can point a film or television camera, but considerable skill is needed to compose an aesthetically pleasing picture. The more complex the medium, the more baffling it is for the ordinary person both to operate and use successfully.

3. Service and maintenance

A basic training course in the operation of equipment must of necessity be fairly limited and is unlikely to equip the class teacher for repairing the film projector or video cassette recorder. He needs either the support of a trained technical assistant who can be quickly summoned when needed or an efficient after-sales service from the manufacturers. Equipment has to be regularly serviced if it is to function efficiently, especially in countries where climatic conditions may adversely affect its performance. Technical education and training systems have to ensure that skilled manpower is available to man service centres, whether provided by manufacturers or users.

D. DENIAL AND CONTROL OF ACCESS

Many powerful radio stations are in daily use beaming political, commercial and ideological messages to distant countries. From 1939 to 1942 propaganda was developed into a weapon of war. Satellite broadcasting opens up the possibilities of radio transmissions reaching farther with less power and television programmes of many nations being available for all who wish to watch. Not unnaturally a number of governments are perturbed by this prospect and possibly political and commercial pressures to deny such access may prove greater than the public's pressure to have it. Plans are already well advanced for the linking of cable networks by national and international satellites.

Cable networks at first sight may appear to provide an easily controllable means of access. Scrambling techniques have already been developed in connexion with Pay-TV systems in order to deny free access to certain programmes for which the viewer is required to pay an extra fee.

Developments of widespread cable networks providing links with computers (e.g. to reduce our dependence on money in business transactions) immediately produce an outcry against a possible misuse and consequent invasion of privacy. Much time and effort is being expended to provide adequate safeguards which will prevent unauthorized access to computer records or possible wire-tapping.

Copyright restrictions are another form of control of access which are in some circumstances tantamount to denial of access. A teacher, for example, may wish to incorporate a film extract or video recording into his own programme but he is hampered by the copyright law. In some countries schools' broadcasts can be recorded within educational institutions, but even that concession is limited in most cases. Reproduction of print is restricted in similar ways. Many existing copyright laws are under revision due to the impact of new copying techniques.

E. BROWSABILITY

Making material available is not the same as providing true access. The missing factor in the equation is the freedom to select, but the selection process itself is a very hit and miss affair without the opportunity to browse. At present print is by far the most browsable medium but even here the new technologies are improving the position still further. While a limited collection of books and journals can already be browsed in some libraries by the use of micro

form copies, their range is now being greatly extended, both in number and kind, to include the books of many libraries and also rare documents not normally on open access.

Audio recordings in either tape or disc form can often be sampled in listening booths in shops but proper browsing is very restricted by the long playing time. What is needed is a means of speeding up the replay without at the same time raising the frequency so that the recording becomes unintelligible. The technology for doing this already exists but has yet to be applied for this purpose.

Video recordings present similar problems of long playing times. If simple speed-up techniques, such as those made possible by some film editing machines, are attempted, the synchronized sound becomes unintelligible. Browsing would be improved by either a specially edited short sequence of selected extracts with accompanying sound or preferably a means of speeding up as required without loosing sound quality or synchronization.

Teachers have shown themselves unwilling to adopt in toto material produced commercially or within another institution. Their training has to include the production of software and the adaption of outside material for their own specific purposes. Yet, how does the teacher decide whether some of the material (e.g. on film), is suitable for his purpose? He cannot quickly check it as he might in the case of a textbook, and certainly the last thing the teacher wants is to face a class without having previewed the material he is going to present. Until this problem is adequately solved the growth rate of the use of non-print material, selected by the user, is unlikely to increase rapidly.

F. ENVIRONMENTAL LIMITATIONS

1. Geographical

The first group of limitations imposed on access to the media by environment are those resulting from the geographical location and the resultant physical conditions. The area to be served and the type of terrain will influence both the distribution of print, film or other recordings and also the size and type of radio or television broadcasting transmitters required. The part of the world in which the service areas are located will also determine the possible bands in the frequency spectrum which such transmitters can use. Any extreme climatic conditions should influence the design of equipment to be used and hence its resultant reliability. In many cases this is likely to prove prohibitively expensive.

2. Degree of development

The degree of development of the service area will produce another group of limitations. The density of population per unit area and the degree of urbanization within it will limit the choice of distribution system for any type of mass media. Without a sufficient concentration of population, items such as daily postal services, telephone and cable networks become far too costly. The existence or absence of road, rail, postal, telephone and broadcasting networks will be an immediate help to or limitation on the potential development of media services for education. Equally important will be the degree of sophistication of the governmental and organizational structures covering the service area. These will have determined the educational system and the degree of co-operation between different bodies serving schools and individual learners (e.g. a public library service if it exists may be quite separate from or closely allied to school and college work). Any but the simplest equipment needs electricity. If no mains electricity is available there is an immediate severe limitation on the equipment which can be used if it has to rely on batteries. Even if mains electricity is available there may still be problems (e.g. equipment designed for the American mains supply will seldom work on European supplies and vice versa).

3. Manpower

Skilled manpower to service and maintain equipment has already been mentioned. Here again the environment will play an important part. If well developed technical college exist in the service area then it is likely that there will be a pool of technicians, craftsmen and artists with basic skills who can easily be trained to service new types of equipment and to prepare materials to be used on it. However, if the appropriate technical education is undeveloped, and this applies to advanced as well as emergent nations, it will take a very long time for the area to produce people skilled to operate and maintain hardware and to produce the related software.

4. Financial

The final group of environmental limitations are those produced by financial considerations. The economic resources of the area, whether determined by natural resources such as mineral deposits or the technological skills of its population, will to a large extent determine the degree of national investment in media productions and distribution, while the wealth of its people as individuals or groups will determine their ability to participate in or use the media. To some people buying a newspaper is still a luxury, while others, given the opportunity, would not balk at the cost of buying their own television camera and video cassette recorder to make their own productions or to store material from a multi-channel network to which their colour television receiver is connected.

The introduction of new techniques is often expensive. Equipment and its software usually costs more than the printed word. Schools, for example, may wish to introduce new techniques but have only a limited amount of money to spend per capita each year, and audio-visual equipment often comes low on the list of priorities. Most schools in countries with established broadcasting systems would like several radio and television sets, but the cost is usually prohibitive. Equipment has to be shared among many users and then organizational problems will be sure to arise.

It is not only the hardware, the large initial outlay, which has to be considered. Many schools have taken the decision to invest money in a video tape recorder, and in the near future many more will buy a video cassette recorder. Frequently they will not have calculated the true cost of tapes, which if they are to be kept for any length of time will soon begin to eat up funds. The total cost likely to result from any innovation should be carefully calculated before the initial decision is taken.

CHAPTER 3

An approach to systems

Improved opportunities for the various types of access described in Chapter 1 are possible as a result of many recent technical developments. These will be described in Chapter 4, but of equal importance is the evolution of a particular set of approaches to planning and management, collectively known as the systems approach, which has facilitated progress, and in some cases actually made it possible.

A.   EARLY HISTORY

Examination of the common usage of the word "system" in such diverse contexts as digestive system, postal system, parliamentary system, leads to a simple definition of a system as a collection of related components (things or people) working together for more or less well-defined purposes.   Thus it is apparent that many different types of individual systems have existed for a very long time.

A significant change occurred at that point in time when there was the first recognition of common elements in the operation of all types of systems.   The occurrence can be dated with a fair degree of accuracy during the period of early work on electronic amplifiers.

Early radio receivers had a very simple circuit added to their thermionic valve amplifiers.   This circuit enabled a small portion of the output to be fed back into the input where it was automatically amplified again.   This circuit was known as a "reaction" or positive feedback circuit (see figure 1).

Increasing the "reaction" produced a louder output, but too much reaction led to instability at which point the quality of the sound would rapidly deteriorate and eventually the receiver would sing, or more accurately, howl.

Later a refinement of the reaction circuit in which a phase invertor was included allowed a portion of the output to be fed back in such a way that it was subtracted from the input (see figure 2). This negative feedback, while reducing the effective amplification, was found to produce greater stability and a number of other benefits.

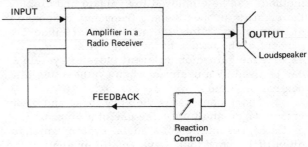

VARIES AMOUNT OF POSITIVE FEEDBACK

Fig. 1 – Positive feedback in a radio receiver

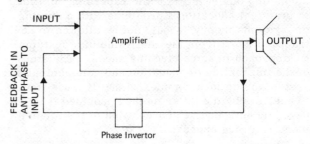

Fig. 2 – Negative feedback

Its introduction is usually attributed to a Canadian engineer named Black and it is possible that surviving references to "black boxes" (e. g. aircraft flight recorders) originate from this source. However, it is certain that Black worked with the eminent mathematician Nyquist who developed a general theory of feedback and established precise criteria for stability which were found to apply to all types of amplifier. The same principles were also found to be applicable to management and economic systems where comparable stability could be expected from the right amount of feedback - a fact anticipated by that keen observer of social systems, Charles Dickens, and demonstrated by Mr. Micawber's solemn warning to David Copperfield to observe "that if a man had twenty pounds a year for his income, and spent nineteen pounds, nineteen shillings and sixpence, he would be happy, but that if he spent twenty pounds one shilling he would be miserable".

In parallel with the investigation into electronic systems the understanding of organic systems developed and further stimulated the idea of a general "systems theory".

B. SYSTEMS THEORY

A complex electro-mechanical control system can be accurately described by a set of differential equations. By a variety of mathematical manipulation and transformation techniques these equations can be converted into one of a number of recognizable mathematical models. Once this has been done a number of well-established methods can be employed to evaluate and display the stability properties and frequency response of the system. Since the processes are independent of the nature of the original system, experience gained on different types of system can be used by a designer when synthesizing his control problems.

In sharp contrast is the very loose and often rather vague and imprecise use of a diagrammatic representation of a social system which is often little more than a systematic or applied common sense approach rather than a true systems approach. The rather common practice of sprinkling otherwise valuable papers on solutions to practical educational problems with a dusting of "systems theory" should not be allowed to detract too much from the real value of a systematic approach in some circumstances. The study of the interaction of education and communication systems is of such complexity that it lends itself to analysis by the latter method provided it is based on an adequate appreciation of the former more rigorous approach.

C. APPLICATIONS

Strictly speaking there is only one universal system of which we ourselves and every thing and person to which we relate are components. However, in practice we can isolate any part of the whole system which we wish to consider. Such a sub-system will have numerous outputs to and inputs from other sub-systems. All these need to be identified and held constant when the performance of the selected system is being investigated to measure its reaction to one controlled variable.

For example the educational system of a country can be divided into many sub-systems such as central and regional education authorities and individual schools. Each school has numerous external connexions, a few of which are illustrated below (see figure 3).

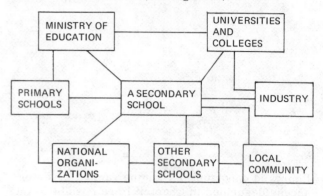

Fig. 3 – A school sub-system

If we wished to study, for example, the financial operation of the school, then the system could perhaps be reduced to a simpler but still valid network with inputs and outputs as shown (see figure 4).

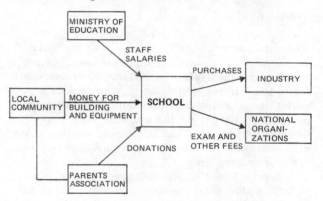

Fig. 4 – A school financial system

D. EFFICIENCY

When discussing the performance of any system involving people in terms of its lack of efficiency, an emotive reaction is common because there is frequently confusion between inefficiency and sloth. Therefore it is important to adhere to the scientific definition:

$$\text{Efficiency} = \frac{\text{Useful Work Output}}{\text{Total Energy Input}}$$

Factors contributing to the loss of efficiency in any system, although not all definable in precise terms, can be identified as:

1. Uncertainty of the true objectives of the system. This uncertainty is apparent even in many examples of hardware, where it is often confused with poor design. In institutional systems new recruits and middle management often fail to appreciate the objectives originally set for an enterprise by its top management.

2. Needless repetition or duplication of some parts or processes in a system. In the design of modern control systems, particularly those involving logic circuits, great attention is paid to improving their efficiency by systematically removing any redundant elements. However, such a conscious effort is seldom apparent in systems employing human components.

3. Some components inappropriate for their purpose or functions. There are innumerable examples of this type of inefficiency in educational systems ranging from overprovision (e.g. a too elaborately equipped television studio) to underprovision, (e.g. a small television receiver being watched by a large class).

    The human components in the same system show a similar range from professional teachers acting as clerks to heads of schools inadequately trained as managers.

4. Friction between components of the system. Any mechanical system from a door hinge to a complete engine works better if oil is provided regularly to prevent unnecessary friction.

    The bearing of an engine shaft which is starved of lubricating oil soon runs dry and hot because the friction between the two parts causes energy to be wasted as heat instead of contributing to the output of the engine. An identical situation can arise between two human components in an institutional system. The energy dissipated in prolonging the animosity between them reduces the energy available for the achievement of the objectives of their institution. Excessive friction can lead to broken links in either case.

5. Broken links - especially communication links. An obvious drop in efficiency, if not a complete breakdown, usually results from a broken linkage in a machine; less apparent and more difficult to measure are the inefficiencies resulting from broken or unmade connexions in telephone systems, while most obscure of all are the inefficiencies resulting from the breakdown of communications between people, particularly those whose professional exchanges should lead to creative developments.

6. Susceptibility to the effects of external noise. In this context, noise is defined as any external influence which has an adverse effect on the operation of the system. The operation of a television system can be very inefficient because electrical interference makes the received picture resemble a scene in a snowstorm Similarly unsolicited and often inappropriate and inaccurate advice can waste the time and energies of those recipients who should be concentrating on the smooth and efficient operation of the system in which they work.

7. Inadequate feedback of the right type to stabilize or improve the system's performance. If an automatic control is required to regulate the temperature of a room, then the feedback to the heating control must be an indication of the difference between the actual and desired room temperature. If the room is too hot the heater must be switched OFF not ON, so the phase of the feedback, or having the right type of feedback is vital. Similarly, a commercial system, for example, would not survive for long if it received inadequate or incorrect feedback on its selling performance.

8. Unsuitable, inadequate or outdated methods, materials or components incorporated in the system. The use of metal guides for the tape on some early helical scan video tape recorders led to many problems before they were replaced by more suitable materials - in this case, ceramic. Comparable problems may arise in systems with human components which are out of date or unsuitable, but the required replacement or updating may not be such a simple task even if the cause of the inefficiency is correctly diagnosed!

    Since an inefficient system is by definition one in which energy is wasted, and energy in whatever form has a monetary value, it follows that improving the efficiency of a system will also make it more acceptable in economic terms. Such considerations are of paramount importance in, for example, the design of a power station and all concerned in the process readily acknowledge the fact. However, in designing most of the parts of an educational system such considerations are seldom mentioned and at best come a very poor second to concerns for effectiveness.

E. EDUCATIONAL TECHNOLOGY

Technology, frequently confused with machines, is better defined as men, machines and materials working together in a system with a known purpose. This leads us to a definition of educational technology as men, machines and materials working together as a system with the purpose of facilitating and enhancing both teaching and learning.

    True technologies which have developed comparatively recently are distinguishable from the craft or early industrial technologies which preceded them by their operational modes. Comparing the model of the aircraft industry in the flying-machine era of the 1930s with that of the 1970s producing Concorde, the working structure of the modern technology emerges as a multi-stage process of which the main elements appear to be:

1. Consideration of the total working environment of the product.

2. Definition of the production objectives.

3. Review of the existing state-of-the-art and where necessary improving materials and methods required for the product.

4. Planning a total system to meet the production objectives.

5. Actual production, starting with prototypes which are tested to provide the first stage of a constant feedback of performance data to effect improvements.

Substituting operation for production in each of the above elements makes the structure more generally applicable as a description of any technology. It can then be applied specifically to education and training.

1. A study of the total environment within which the educational process has to operate is crucial to educators in both developing and developed countries. It is just as important for teachers to appreciate the difficulties arising from the lack of information and experience in developing countries, as it is for those in developed countries to appreciate the vast input of information from the mass media which every child has in addition to that which he receives in school and college - the process which the French call l'école parallèle.

2. Whilst the general aims of education are seldom in dispute, it is still comparatively rarely that specific objectives have been set for an educational process. However the production of an educational programme, whether in the sense of television or of programmed instruction, demands precision in the setting of objectives.

Such precision is more commonly found in training situations where precise objectives can be set for the acquisition of specific skills.

3. Various national and international agencies carry out "state-of-the-art" surveys in particular areas from time to time but the process is often rather haphazard and at best the results percolate slowly to those who can most usefully profit from them. The design and development of new methods and materials in education lags far behind most industrial technologies. When one compares the percentage of total expenditure devoted to research and development in education with that put to the same purpose in the electronics industry, it is obvious that the latter will have a development rate many times faster than that of education.

4. Planning a total system is a piece of teamwork which automatically throws light on bad practices. Systems engineers working as a team avoided previous compartmentalization and were able to use the same liquid to drive the engines, cool the cabin and correct the flying trim of the Concorde. Similar principles, applied to the design of a secondary school curriculum have led to the removal of rigid subject barriers.

5. A practical system properly designed to meet an agreed set of educational objectives will almost certainly consist of a judicious mix of media and methods. Too often time or economic pressures restrict the number of methods or media used.

The system should also be planned to give an appropriate degree of feedback so that the mix itself and its individual components can be optimized. The feedback path, if present at all in existing educational systems, is likely to be extremely tenuous. Surprisingly, even expensive educational television programmes which are transmitted over national networks are very seldom pilot tested.

Many educators react against educational technology simply because it is based on the same thought processes as are applicable to creating the model of industrial technology. The emotive reaction, however carefully disguised, usually incorporates some reference to education being concerned with people rather than a factory production-line for inanimate objects: this is followed by a plea for "effectiveness" to be given precedence over "efficiency". Their criteria for effectiveness, in addition to "achievement of agreed objectives", usually include satisfaction with the learning process and growth, development or enhancement of one or more of an individual or group's desirable characteristics.

None of these criteria preclude the idea that more consideration should be given to efficiency, since anything which is efficient must by definition also be effective. However, the converse is not automatically true.

F. FUTURE INTERPLAY BETWEEN EDUCATION AND COMMUNICATION SYSTEMS

Within educational sub-systems the products of communications technology already play a number of important rôles in:

(a) production and presentation of learning material, e.g. film and television;

(b) selection and management of learning resources, e.g. various forms of computer aided learning;

(c) feedback and assessment processes, e.g. feedback classrooms and computer assisted marking.

Perhaps the most important element in the development of educational systems will be providing the learner with ready access to all the resources for learning which he needs. The newer electronic and visual media are of such importance that the educational system must include ready access to them for every learner or learning group.

CHAPTER 4

The means of access

A variety of technical developments, in a number of different fields, have had their impact upon the problem of access. These developments are not necessarily new discoveries but often amount to a new application of a known technique, leading to a novel approach or a change of scale in existing developments. These technical developments can conveniently be classified by the types of facilities which they provide.

A. ACTUAL OR EFFECTIVE INCREASE IN CHANNEL SPACE FOR TRANSMISSION OF INFORMATION

Information, as used here, is the engineer's term for anything which can be converted into an electronic signal. Examples in general order of increasing quantity or complexity are data, sound, still pictures, moving pictures.

1. By the use of higher frequencies for broadcasting

Broadcast frequencies are limited; the search for channel space to accommodate more and more transmissions have caused broadcast engineers to explore ever higher frequencies. Many radio services already use a single-side-band system of modulation which means that they occupy only half the bandwidth which was required by the double-side-band systems that they replace. Despite this, radio broadcasting has virtually exhausted the available space on medium, high and very high frequency bands. Television broadcasting is already using a considerable proportion of the available space in the very, ultra and super high frequency bands. At UHF the terrain has considerable influence on the range of a transmission so that a high degree of area coverage may require the use of many small secondary transmitters. The SHF band theoretically has extensive bandwidth but technical factors restrict its usefulness for broadcasting.

2. By use of multi-channel fixed networks

Access to a number of radio or television channels can be provided by the installation of a cable link between the source and the receiver. Multi-channel capacity can be achieved either by providing separate circuits for each channel or by modulating each channel's signal on to a slightly different carrier frequency.

With systems that use separate circuits, each circuit can be taken to the receiver where a simple selector switch is provided; however, for more than 10-12 circuits this becomes uneconomic. A preferable arrangement is one comparable with the normal telephone network in which a single circuit is provided for each receiver with a dialling system to connect it to a selected channel via an elementary form of exchange fed by trunk circuits.

Systems in which each channel is modulated on to different carrier frequencies, all passing along a single circuit, require a tuning device to select the desired channel. Theoretically, a large number of channels could be provided in this way, but practical systems seldom have more than ten.

Super high frequencies (also known as microwaves) are beginning to be used to carry very large numbers of channels via pipe-like waveguides from one main population centre to another. Even higher frequencies, viz. those in the visible spectrum, are now being brought into use for communication channels. In such systems a laser light beam passing through an optical glass fibre is modulated to carry the required information.

3. By the use of satellites

Where one large region cannot be covered by a single transmitter, it has to be divided into a number of areas so arranged that adjacent areas are served by transmitters working on different frequencies. An economy in frequency space is achieved when a single orbiting satellite transmitter is used to cover the whole region.

As with cable and other fixed networks, the trend in satellite communications is towards ever greater channel capacity. Since "Telstar" in 1962 with its 12 telephone circuits, progress has been very rapid; in 1968 "Intelsat III" was launched with a capacity of 1,200 telephone circuits, while its successor "Intelsat IV" has a capacity equivalent to 5,000 telephone circuits. These satellites are all point-to-point relay rather than broadcasting satellites and work at frequencies below 10 GHz which they share with terrestrial microwave radio-relay systems. Since they are all of relatively low power they demand large receiving aerials and sensitive receivers at the earth stations.

All satellite transmitters depend upon solar energy for their operation. A transmitter of sufficient power suitable for broadcasting direct to individual homes would therefore require a very large number of solar-cells to produce the electrical energy needed. This in turn means that the satellite has to be large and heavy and as a result more expensive to build and launch.

Broadcasting satellites will operate in the 12 GHz band or at higher frequencies. Satellites such as the Canadian CTS to be launched in 1975, have two important characteristics in the context of this discussion viz; (a) a limited number of channels operating from any given satellite; and (b) a very large area of the earth being covered by radiated signals. If used in Europe, for example, to provide national services to each country, each would have four or five channels for its own use.

An intermediate stage between the current relay operations and projected direct broadcasting to individual domestic receivers involves the use of slightly more elaborate receiving aerials and receivers in order to reduce the transmitter power requirements. Such receiving systems can reasonably be installed to serve institutions, community viewing centres, blocks of flats or to feed a small cable distribution system to a group of homes. Experiments with this type of satellite operation are either planned or in operation in parts of Canada, United States, Latin America, India and Africa.

4. By the use of information compression or injection techniques

Recent developments have produced an effective economy in channel or frequency space (a) by techniques which compress the information to be transmitted into a narrower bandwidth; or (b) by techniques which superimpose additional information on to a normal signal waveform; or (c) a combination of (a) and (b).

These include, in the case of television, possibilities of inserting the sound or complete "pages" of alpha-numeric information into the synchronizing pulses which are always a part of the transmitted signal. In West Germany, a system using an analogue time-compression technique enables up to 12 audio signals, with bandwidths of 13 kHz, to be transmitted during the vertical synchronizing pulse of a television signal.

5. By the use of recorders

There is now a whole range of new, cheap, easy-to-use recording devices for both sound and vision which, because of the relatively low cost of making the recordings, provide an alternative to broadcasting or cable transmission by introducing the possibility of reaching a large audience by way of distributed software. Such a process, since it is independent of the constraints of channel space, is, in the context of this discussion, equivalent to the provision of unlimited channel space.

6. By the use of the latent capacity in existing systems

Although actual or effective extra channel capacity can be made available by any of the means described above, there are many examples to be found where the capacity of the existing transmission or distribution networks is not fully used.

Many existing cable systems were installed to facilitate reception of broadcast programmes either in a weak signal area or from a single aerial. The initials CATV, widely used in North America, originally stood for "community antenna television". The fact that they are now also used to represent cable television is indicative of a change of operation in some places. Such cable networks often have spare capacity which is interlinked to provide new channels for purposes such as locally produced education or community programmes.

National and regional radio and television broadcasting transmitters, particularly in developing countries, are often inoperative for a significant part of each day. In the United Kingdom, for example, there is at present spare capacity during the day time on the second BBC television channel and during the night hours on all channels. This extra capacity could be used for minority programming or, with the introduction of automatic video recorders, dark-hours broadcasting could be used, for example, for educational purposes.

B.   FEEDBACK PATHS

1.   Dial-access

One particular use of a feedback path is more correctly related to the previous section, i.e. when a control or selection path is added, usually for dialling in a number to a central control or exchange point, the feedback provides the user with the freedom to select one of a theoretically unlimited number of alternatives which he wishes to connect to his receiver via his single input path.   The process is analogous to the operation of the telephone system in which each subscriber can be connected to any one of millions of information sources (i.e. other subscribers).

2.   Broadcasts

For many years feedback to radio or television broadcasts was only possible via a completely different medium - written correspondence - making the process indistinguishable from readers' letters to newspapers. Then phone-ins to live programmes were made possible by engineering developments which eliminated the possibility of positive feedback such as often occurs when a speaker using a public address system takes the microphone too near a loudspeaker and causes the system to become unstable and start howling. Recent developments now permit a greater number of participants and provide greater reliability than in the past, with the result that this type of programme is far more common, particularly in the output of local radio stations. Improvements in VHF and UHF portable, short-range, two-way radio links of the superior walkie-talkie type and slightly larger installations suitable for cars, boats and helicopters, have obviated the need for telephone lines. Direct injection into live programmes is now possible from such sources.

Although expensive television cameras of broadcast quality, with associated microwave transmitters, all small enough to be carried by one man, are coming into use for on-the-spot reporting of such things as public reaction to an event featured in a news broadcast.

3.   Cable networks

Groups who are keen to gain access to community television systems frequently think in terms of feeding responses back into the system from the receiving point. It is relevant therefore to point out that feedback is impossible along many existing cable networks because of the design of the line amplifiers. Where it is possible, the bandwidth is severely limited in most of the older installations, and in consequence would only be sufficient for data pulses or an audio signal. However, in new, specially designed cable networks, such as those in the Villes Nouvelles in France, filter-amplifier systems have been used which provide a bandwidth on the feedback path sufficient to carry three television channels simultaneously.

Perhaps the most important feedback is of the data type which now extends from push-buttons in feedback classrooms enabling students to indicate their response to multi-choice questions, through programmed learning machines of varying complexity, to teletype and light-pen terminals connected back to computers which enable students to participate in a new type of Socratic dialogue.

If data feedback is applied to a cable system, receiving points must be provided with a device having some form of keyboard similar to those found on touch-tone telephones or small electronic desk calculators. This keyboard could have either a simple numeric or a more complex alphanumeric layout. The device would normally also contain a small data storage unit so that complete messages can be fed back very rapidly to some form of computer in the network centre.

A simple numeric feedback device will allow the user to be identified by the network centre when he sends his own terminal number. He can then send a series of pulses which indicate his responses to questions.   A simple system of this type would enable the following type of activity:

(a)   Selection of:
  (i)   available broadcast radio and television programmes;
  (ii) special programmes from a video library;
  (iii) information, such as sport or entertainment calendars, library catalogues, medical and health advice, stock exchange prices, travel time-tables, weather and traffic reports, etc.;
  (iv) education programmes for home study.
(b)   Response to:
  (i)   multi-choice test questions forming part of programmed instruction in home study educational courses;
  (ii) questions forming the basis of commercial market research or an official

opinion poll or even voting in an election;
(iii) shopping lists by ordering from a special catalogue or in response to advertisements;
(iv) automatic requests emanating from a central recording computer calling for readings from the user's electricity and fuel meters. These responses could also be automated, and eventually lead to a fully automatic reading and charging system;
(v) participation in interactive games by those who are housebound.

(c) Alarms

Automatic fire or burglar alarms could operate by way of the feedback path.

C. CHEAP AND EASY TO OPERATE PRODUCTION FACILITIES

Broadcasting, particularly television broadcasting, has for many years been an expensive process which could be undertaken only by a wealthy public corporation or a successful commercial organization. Studio cameras and video recorders cost tens of thousands of dollars but the rapid development of closed-circuit systems in schools, colleges, hospitals and industry has stimulated design of smaller, more portable and very much less expensive equipment.

Initially, the technical quality of such equipment was far inferior to that used by the broadcasters. A number of technical developments are now bringing this type of equipment very near to the standards which are acceptable for public broadcasting or transmission over cable networks.

The video equipment developed for use in industry and educational institutions had of necessity to be operable by personnel whose expertise lay in fields other than television. Now that simpler studios are being used for closed-circuit operations on private networks within colleges, police and education authorities, etc., production processes have to be carried out by small numbers of omnicompetent technicians instead of the range of highly trained specialists which most broadcasters would employ. The portable outside broadcasting equipment of such closed-circuit network operators is also a scaled-down and simplified version of that used by broadcasters for the same purposes. It is the appearance of this type of equipment on the open market which has stimulated the growth of many amateur video groups representing community associations and action groups of all types. The products of such groups range from the moving equivalent of the worst type of holiday snapshots that no stranger should ever be forced to view, to stimulating, professional quality documentaries which are a

real challenge to established producers and directors. The problem which many such groups face is that of finding an audience for their programmes, which means in practice finding a transmission or distribution system willing to accept their recordings. Other groups, however, are quite content to replay their recordings immediately to a small viewing group which forms a part of the community with which they are working or to some comparable group as a stimulus. For such groups television is a social tool which they use deliberately as a catalyst to generate community interest and action.

D. STORAGE, SELECTION AND RETRIEVAL SYSTEMS

1. Storage

The storage of information in a readily accessible form is a major problem of the twentieth century. Traditional libraries are finding it increasingly difficult to keep pace with the publication of new material - and material which is appearing in an ever increasing amount in non-book form. Problems of storage space have already forced some libraries to adopt some form of micro copying for books and journals.

Another approach has been the use of computers and their magnetic tape or disc stores. Already in existence are examples of vast information data banks. The information so shared is still largely of the alpha-numeric type, although sometimes diagrams are also stored and recent developments permitting the conversion of television signals into digital form will enable colour moving pictures to be stored in a computer's memory bank.

2. Selection

The selection of required information from the continually multiplying and diversifying store of knowledge presents great problems even to trained librarians with the benefit of modern abstracting techniques. A full-scale search in a reasonably short time would be very difficult without computer assistance.

The new technologies are being introduced at all levels. The local library now has its catalogues on computer produced microfilm and with the aid of a simple reader the borrower can quickly locate material in his field of interest. In some cases, where the collection of material is small, catalogues of other libraries in the area are incorporated, thus expanding the range of material available. Services provided by public libraries can be far more detailed. The reader who is interested in any specific area within a subject can ask his librarian to produce a list of material. At present this facility is not on-line and the reader has to wait a day or two for searches to be done, but as abstracting and cataloguing services improve and selection facilities keep pace with these developments information will become instantly available.

As the public library systems grow larger, which seems to be inevitable, telecommunications facilities will become increasingly important. In some areas, such as education, it is unlikely that instant retrieval facilities will be needed, but certainly a network will be required which can supply bibliographic information with the minimum delay.

Research libraries, especially in the medical and industrial fields are installing high speed links for both selection from bibliographic information and retrieval of specific items. In Sweden, for example, computers in research libraries are linked, with terminals usually situated in university libraries. Links are being built up between member nations of the European Space Organisation and in the United States there are already approximately 30 systems where computers have been interconnected. Regional networks to link computers are being set up in the United Kingdom - but costs are high.

International agreement on the format of bibliographic data is an essential prerequisite to information selection. Fortunately, it has been found possible to develop a format for non-book materials from that used for computerized book cataloguing in the United Kingdom and North America, the MARC format (machine readable catalogue). This standard format is being developed to permit the provision of all multi-media documentation.

Under the auspices of the Council for Educational Technology for the United Kingdom, a committee, working closely with the newly formed British Library, is setting up a central agency to handle the technical and control problems of a national documentation system. The MARC system developed by the British National Bibliography is being used to create computer records of both book and non-book materials. When given a cataloguing requirement the machine selects the relevant records, sequences them and sets them up in specified type face and lay-out, makes up columns, pages and indexes and delivers a set of films from which a printer can print and bind copies of the catalogue. The machine can also produce cheap microfilm print-out[1]. Any information stored in the computer can be selected as required and entries amended or deleted. If a suitable computer is available, individual organizations can have copies of the input tape for their own use. Media catalogues produced so far in the United Kingdom using these techniques

include those of the British National Film Catalogue, the British Universities' Film Catalogue and CET's own HELPIS (Higher Education Learning Programmes Information Service) catalogue.

3. Retrieval

Retrieval of selected material produces further problems for the user. Although in many spheres there is little evidence that the user wants or needs instant retrieval of an item, in other areas, such as medical records, instant information is essential. A number of feasibility studies on limited areas have shown on a small scale how the retrieval problem might be tackled with computer assistance. However, the sheer magnitude of the problem of providing access to a reasonable proportion of the growing total of knowledge will demand something more radical in terms of technical innovation than the stringing together of television type terminals, computer controls and magnetic disc or tape storage of literal and visual information.

Experiments are being carried out in a number of places on interactive, two-way communication systems which allow the user to request information and to indicate his response via push-buttons or verbally.

Britain's Ceefax and Oracle systems will allow the public to receive a continuous information service on conventional broadcast television networks. If a similar system were developed for cable networks there would be more opportunity for individuals to have access to the particular information they required.

In the United States several systems of information retrieval are being piloted. The Mitre Corporation has built and demonstrated in Reston, Virginia a two-way system using the Time-shared Interactive Computer - Controlled Information Television (TICCIT). It is proposed to install the system in Washington where a Cable Television System is being introduced (see Appendix page 54 for details of TICCIT).

Another elaborate, specially designed network in which the computer plays an even greater part is the Programmed Logic for Automatic Teaching Operations (PLATO) development based on the University of Illinois. The current system, known as PLATO IV, is being expanded to serve several thousand specially designed user terminals. These interactive computer graphics terminals each have an $8\frac{1}{2}''$ square flat glass plasma panel with 512 x 512 individual digitally addressable light points under computer control

(1) L. A. Gilbert: A British Documentation System for Non-book Materials. Educational Media International, October 1973.

giving a capability of displaying more than 2,000 characters. Up to 1,000 terminals can be connected by a simple television channel. Extensive central computer core storage allows rapid access to large amounts of material for use by either (a) students following courses written to accommodate individual rates and styles of learning or (b) teachers writing and editing new material to add to the library of thousands of lessons which is already available. Auxillary equipment, controllable by the computer, can be added to a terminal to provide audio systems, touch panels, film and slide projection, etc. (see Appendix, page 50 for details of PLATO).

The data retrieval problem can be greatly simplified if the storage can be moved away from the central computer to the terminal units around the periphery of the system. This arrangement has the advantage that it loads the computer and hence the communication network, very lightly. Such a system is in use in the United Kingdom with the high density terminal stores in the form of X 150 optical magnification ultrafiche with an edge pattern on each page. Logical functions are carried out by the central computer which sends a digital signal to any selected terminal and can thereby select, in a few seconds, one out of hundreds of thousands of pages. Storage costs are also low - about $1 for 5,000 pages.

CHAPTER 5

Technological developments

A. UNDERLYING DEVELOPMENTS

Before looking at recent developments in media production, recording and transmission equipment and concentrating particularly on those which affect access, an attempt will be made to sketch in the general electronic technology background against which these developments should be seen.

Cause and effect are often difficult to separate in this area but there can be little doubt that the development of such well-known things as computers, artificial satellites and manned space probes have had a considerable affect on some of the less well-known, yet still fundamental processes involved in electronic controls and communications upon which they themselves are so heavily dependent. The need to reduce size, weight and electrical energy consumption and also to increase quality and reliability of control and communication systems has led to many changes of which the following are a selection:

1. Valves to transistors to integrated circuits to large-scale integration

In the 1950s a world-wide submarine cable network linked up national telephone networks; extensive radio services and several television services were in use. All were entirely dependent upon the thermionic valve to provide the required signals, amplification, modulation, switching, etc.

Invented in 1948, the transistor was, by the mid-1960s, the mainspring of advances in the telecommunications and other industries. It has produced savings in space, weight, power and cost, and has greatly improved reliability and portability. Whereas valve amplifiers suffered from ageing, which necessitated frequent checking to readjust gain and balance, transistors do not require such testing at all. The valve-type amplifiers on inter-city telephone trunk routes required a special repeater station every 5 km. to house the amplifiers which had to have a lethal 1,000 volt supply. Comparable transistor-type amplifiers need no repeater station and work from safe low voltages.

The transistor's impact on the computer industry has been equally dramatic but as computer technology has developed, so has the demand for vast numbers of similar circuits, each typically containing a pair of transistors and a few passive components. At the same time there has been a growing requirement to perform millions of calculations, albeit quite simple ones, every second. Since an electric current cannot move along a wire faster than the speed of light (300,000 kilometres/second), in one nanosecond i. e. $\dfrac{\text{one second}}{1,000,000,000}$ it would only travel about 30 cm. Thus when very high speed calculations are needed the time taken by an electric current to move from one circuit to another becomes very significant. This problem stimulated the research and development which has produced the modern integrated circuit. The ideas used in the parallel developments of printed circuit boards, now universally used as a better alternative to separately wiring every circuit component, combined with the use of semiconductor materials from which transistors are constructed, have made it possible by photographic techniques to put thousands of complete circuits on to a tiny chip of silicon which is barely visible to the naked eye. Such devices are now referred to as large-scale integration (LSI) to distinguish them from earlier devices combining a small group of circuits. The distances travelled by the electric currents performing the computations are then so small that the rate of computation can be greatly increased.

2. Analogue to digital

Perhaps the biggest single change which is sweeping through all aspects of electronic engineering is that from analogue to digital techniques. A few years ago all amplifiers accepted at the input a voltage which was analogous with some varying physical quantity, such as the shape of a sound wave, and produced at the output another larger voltage which was still a more or less faithful reproduction or analogy of the input. Starting with computers that worked entirely with simple ON/OFF or YES/NO pulse circuits, digital techniques have been developed and from them coding techniques which allow any continuously varying physical quanity, such as a sound wave, to be represented by a varying series of numbers. These numbers represent the amplitude of the wave at each time that it is sampled.

The change to pulse code modulation (PCM)) digital techniques for the transmission and switching of signals over telephone networks is already well advanced. For satisfactory transmission of speech amplitude samples have to be taken 8,000 times a second. Each sample is then represented by combinations of 8 ON or OFF pulses which can define $2^8 = 256$ levels of amplitude. Thus a single speech channel must transmit $8 \times 8,000 = 64,000$ ON/OFF digital pulses or bits per second. (The YES or NO, ON or OFF pulse is the binary digit or the smallest possible bit of information and therefore pulse rates are often measured in BITS PER SECOND.) PCM is a vital element in the planned development of most large-capacity transmission systems for the future, whether they employ coaxial cables, waveguides, microwave relays, satellites or optical fibres.

Other computer derived digital techniques have produced high-speed logic devices which can effectively take a logical switching "decision" every nanosecond.

All television camera tubes currently in use in studios produce a voltage analogue of the varying shades they see as they scan the scene before them. It is only in research and development laboratories that television cameras which produce a digital output are found at present. Perhaps for this reason television engineers were initially slow to use digital methods but very rapid advances are now being made to convert as many television processes as possible to digital techniques. A particularly significant achievement is the conversion of an American 525 line 60 Hz type colour picture to a British 625 line 50 Hz type colour picture. This was done by converting the American television signal, received by satellite, into digital form, feeding it into a computer programme to produce an appropriate digital output based on British Standards which after conversion back to analogue form produced a picture identical to the original.

The use of digital techniques in television is also making it possible to perform new "tricks", some of which may be of interest to the education world. One example is the digital control tracks added to video tape recordings to facilitate the identification and location of individual frames. Although primarily intended to simplify editing, the process can also make it possible to display or extract specific shots or sequences for educational purposes. A second example is found in the use of pulse code modulation techniques superimposed on other types of signal. It has been possible for some while to "hide" programme sound, after first converting it into a digital form, in gaps in the television signal. It is now possible to "hide" complete "pages" of information in these gaps and to give viewers whose television receiver has a small extra unit the chance to extract them and read them.

3. Moving up the frequency spectrum

As the total quantity of information, in whatever form, has increased, so also has the demand for frequency space in which to transmit it. Whether for broadcasting or conducted transmission along some sort of predetermined path the demand is always for more bandwidth. As the lower frequencies in the electromagnetic wave spectrum are used up the required bandwidth can only be found by continually moving farther up the frequency spectrum. As the spectrum diagram below reminds us (see figure 1) electromagnetic waves, which all have the same characteristics, except for their frequency or wavelength, are commonly divided into discrete bands. However, as we have already seen, the waves of different bands are increasingly used for similar purposes.

Each octave (i.e. doubling of top frequency) that has been won has been at the cost of long and intensive research and development not only in the fields of propagation characteristics and transmission media but also in the equally difficult fields of new types of amplifiers, modulators etc., to work at each new higher frequency.

(a) Very high frequencies (VHF 30-300 MHz) are used both for direct broadcasting for radio and television (the latter occupying up to 13 channels in Europe - theoretically more channels could be developed but in practice most of the frequency space is already occupied, e.g. by a radio navigation system) and also for coaxial cable television systems of nine or more channels. Frequencies in the VHF band are also used for trunk telephone coaxial cable links. These use a system called frequency division multiplexing (FDM), which allows groups of channels to be

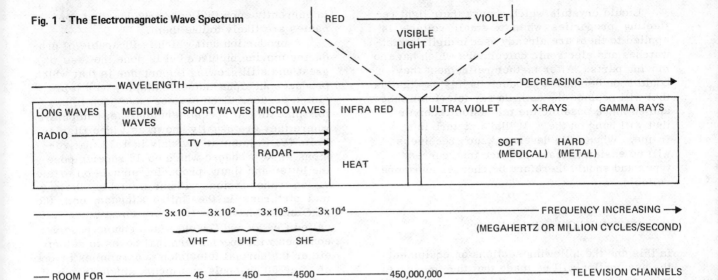

Fig. 1 – The Electromagnetic Wave Spectrum

LONG WAVES	MEDIUM WAVES	SHORT WAVES	MICRO WAVES	INFRA RED		ULTRA VIOLET	X-RAYS	GAMMA RAYS
RADIO		TV	RADAR	HEAT		SOFT (MEDICAL)	HARD (METAL)	

WAVELENGTH ⸺⸺⸺⸺⸺⸺⸺⸺⸺ DECREASING ⟶

VISIBLE LIGHT — RED ⸺⸺⸺ VIOLET

⸺ 3×10 ⸺ 3×10² ⸺ 3×10³ ⸺ 3×10⁴ ⸺⸺⸺⸺ FREQUENCY INCREASING ⟶
(MEGAHERTZ OR MILLION CYCLES/SECOND)

VHF   UHF   SHF

⸺ ROOM FOR ⸺⸺ 45 ⸺ 450 ⸺ 4500 ⸺⸺ 450,000,000 ⸺⸺ TELEVISION CHANNELS

combined into progressively larger groups (e.g. 12 up to 2,700 audio channels) before transmission over the main routes.

(b) Ultra high frequency (UHF 300-3,000 MHz). This band of frequencies is now extensively used for television broadcasting (e.g. in the United Kingdom it provides a nation-wide 4-channel capability, although due to the limited range of these frequencies, hundreds of low-power repeater transmitters will be needed to provide more than 96% coverage of the population).

(c) Super high frequencies (SHF above 3,000 MHz). Waves of these frequencies are also known as microwaves and the wavelengths range from several millimetres down to fractions of a millimetre. When used for open air radiation their range is strictly line-of-sight and they are considerably affected by atmospheric conditions, particularly rain. However, they can be guided by either rectangular or circular cross-section pipes called waveguides. These pipes have extremely critical mechanical tolerances. Devising methods of making long lengths with sufficient accuracy has kept several teams of research and development engineers busy for the past few years. To achieve success complex combinations of precision steel tubing with copper wire helices and suitable insulating materials have had to be produced. In addition to work on the guides themselves, much effort has gone into the development of microwave generators and special transistors to work amplifying and other circuits at these extremely high frequencies.

(d) Visible light frequencies. Moving up to even higher frequencies the development of lasers, which are coherent light emitting sources, and the means of modulating their output has opened up new possibilities of very wide band transmission paths. For example a recently announced laser modulator, which incidentally is of ex-

tremely small size, is capable of modulating on to a single laser beam of red light 25,000 radio or 20 television programmes. Since light beams can be completely cut by fog or snow, development has concentrated on guiding these light waves along optical fibre cables. By the use of ultra-pure glass or low-loss liquids inside fine glass tubes the attenuation of the transmitted signal can now be kept very low. A complete cable having 50 conductors with all the necessary padding and protection is only 1 cm. in diameter. It is much cheaper than a comparable cable using copper; it is also mechanically flexible and therefore capable of being laid round bends and in existing ducts.

4. Miniaturization and solid-state techniques

The development of integrated circuits for speeding up computer operations has been described in the first section of this chapter. Similar microelectronic circuits are being applied in a number of communication systems, where they play an essential part in dramatically reducing both the size and the initial cost of the equipment. Because of the greater reliability of microelectronic circuits, running costs - particularly maintenance costs - are also minimized.

As well as their use in amplifying and switching circuits, solid-state devices (a term describing all items in which there are no electrons moving in a gas or vacuum) are being developed for a number of important sensing and display units.

The solid-state television camera is already under development in manufacturers' laboratories. One such camera which has the normal tube replaced by a quarter-inch chip of silicon on which there are some 10,000 pairs of sensors is very small and weighs less than one pound.

Liquid crystals which change their light reflecting properties when a small voltage is applied to them are already used in digital wristwatches and electronic calculators which have no moving parts. After further refinement they could soon be used to produce the display matrix that will replace the cathode ray television tube and so make possible the television receiver that will hang on the wall like a picture in a frame. When fully developed such receivers will be easier to mass produce than current types and should therefore be cheaper and more reliable.

B. PRODUCTION EQUIPMENT

In this and the following sections on equipment the assumption will be made that the "message" to be produced, recorded, transmitted etc., will be of the most demanding type (i.e. will consist of a moving colour picture with accompanying sound). Any exceptions will be specially noted.

The first problem used to be to get enough light in the right place to provide adequate illumination of scene or subject. Two developments have virtually removed this problem. First, where artificial illumination is necessary for film or television, use can now be made of reliable, lightweight, long-life units employing gas discharge tubes, particularly of the tungsten halogen and quartz iodine types, which produce several times as much light per watt as the older incandescent lamps. Secondly, improvements in television camera tubes have so increased sensitivity that they can operate successfully at very low light levels equivalent to twilight or semi-darkness.

Film cameras using the Super 8mm format are now capable of producing picture quality better than that obtained from many 16mm cameras a few years ago. Colour film stock has increased in speed and now uses a thinner base which allows a greater length of film to be accommodated in a given size of spool or cartridge.

Electronic colour cameras used to be large and needed 3 or 4 tubes, and they also required considerable technical skill for setting-up and control. Recently studio colour cameras have become almost completely automatic in setting-up and control processes. Other developments, mainly by Japanese manufacturers, have produced acceptable colour cameras whose weight has been reduced to such an extent that they can now be considered as truly portable and comparable with 16mm film cameras for news gathering. A 3-tube camera weighing 20 lbs and a single-tube camera weighing only 14 lbs, both weights including zoom lenses and mounts, are now commerically available, although their cost

is currently such that only broadcasting companies are likely to use them.

A production unit which is incapable of producing moving pictures but is none the less of great and still growing importance is that which produces an alpha-numeric display on a television screen. Such devices have been in use for some time as special terminals for computers where they are usually known as Video Display Units (VDUs), but it was only in 1973 that versions were produced which could superimpose the letter and figure producing signals on to television transmissions without disturbing the normal pictures. In the United Kingdom both the BBC and IBA have developed systems respectively called Ceefax and Oracle which enable receivers equipped with special terminal boxes to select either the normal television programmes or one of some 50 channels on which a single frame of information is presented. Recently a national technical standard was agreed which will in future be used by both the BBC and the Independent Broadcasting Authority. This standard allows each "page" of information to contain 24 rows of 40 characters (i.e. about 190 words). Various refinements can be added to the system such as upper and lower case letters, simple diagrams, up to six colours and a local input to the terminal box which itself will probably be incorporated into some future television receiver models.

C. RECORDING EQUIPMENT

1. Audio recorders

In the 1930s and 1940s equipment for the production of original gramophone records was in quite common use, extending from portable machines used by reporters and correspondents to those found in seaside resorts as a diversion for the visitors who were willing to pay for the thrill of hearing the "real" sound of their own voices. Such recorders were not intended for copying and the discs once cut could not be reused for another recording.

Nowadays practically all gramophone records are mass produced in very sophisticated and costly industrial pressing plants. By the use of slower rotation speeds and narrower grooves combined with lighter and more sensitive pick-ups, the playing time of records has been increased and the quality improved. However, by their design they are intended only to be played and all domestic record players are strictly replay-only machines.

Reel-to-reel recorders using magnetic tape were first used for audio recording. Rapid improvements in both their record/replay heads and the associated electronic circuits soon made them preferable to gramophone recorders for all but mass copying applications, particularly as they had the added advantage that the recording tape could be erased and reused many times.

2.   Video recorders

It was a natural development to extend the use of magnetic tape recording into the video field. However if the commonly used 1/4" audio tape had been used to store the much greater quantity of information constituting a television signal, the tape would have needed to pass the single recording head at over a hundred miles per hour. This also implies that to "write" all the information needed to reproduce an hour's television programme would require 100 miles of 1/4" tape.   The effective writing speed was therefore increased by using four recording heads moving across the tape 1,500 times per minute and the writing space was increased by using 2" tape. With these changes the tape could then move between the spools at the more moderate and now standard speed of 15 inches per second used by all broadcasters.

The use of video recorders would probably have long been restricted to broadcasting companies, who could afford the large and expensive transverse-scan quadruplex machines, if there had not been further developments in recording techniques.

With 1/2", 3/4" and 1" wide tapes wrapping in a single helical turn around a central drum, it was possible to have a record/replay head or heads spinning at high speeds inside the drum and thus following a long slanting track over the tape as it passed from spool to spool.

This helical-scan system is the basis of all non-broadcast video recorders. A few manufacturers are producing more sophisticated helical-scan machines and have begun to break into the broadcasting market in competition with transverse-scan machines which cost approximately twice as much.

3.   Cassette recorders

The use of audio recorders has risen rapidly with the introduction of compact cassettes.   These provided both a machine which was very much simpler to use than an equivalent reel-to-reel version and also the possibility of a standardized, cheap, easy to handle format for the recordings which has stimulated commercial production, leading to much wider use such as the introduction of audio recordings into libraries.

Video cassette recorders, while still using the helical-scan arrangement, offer similar advantages over comparable reel-to-reel video machines. It is, however, unfortunate that there are already several different formats and standardization now seems unlikely.

4.   Video systems - replay only
(a)   Discs

Many video recording systems have similar characteristics to the gramophone in that they require large and expensive mass copying plant to produce permanent good quality but cheap recordings intended for use by the customers on replay-only machines.   The nearest equivalents are the several video disc systems which use a variety of techniques to pack the necessary information into the relatively small area available.

One system, used by broadcasters for instant replay during football matches, etc., employs a technique of recording on to a disc of magnetic material similar to those used for some computer memories.

A second system uses what is in effect a direct extension of gramophone recording techniques.   The plastic discs, which are obtained by pressings from a metal master, have a large number of very fine grooves.   Replay is achieved by mechnically tracking a pressure stylus across the disc which is rotated at speeds far higher than those used for a gramophone record.

Three more systems have a common element in that each uses a laser beam or beams to produce the master recording.   In the first of these, six tracks are produced on 35mm film which is then converted photographically into a narrow track on a glass master disc.   Photographic contact-printing from the master on to plastic-based discs then follows.   This is a rapid process and the very cheap discs thus produced can be read by photo-transistors in a relatively simple and cheap player.

In the second example, a laser beam is used to produce a spiral pattern of dots on a transparent disc coated with a very fine-grain photographic emulsion.   The signal modulation is recorded by varying the diameter and the density of the dots produced.   The replay unit uses a 25 watt lamp to produce a magnified image which is then read by three phototransistors.

In the third example, a laser beam is directed at a glass disc which has a photo-resistive coating.   It penetrates the coating and etches a series of tiny slots in the glass which correspond to the applied modulation.   Plastic disc copies of the glass master are made by conventional gramophone-disc pressing techniques.   In the player a low-power laser and a photo-transistor are used to read the dots.   The laser reading head is electromechanically tracked across the disc but the exact position of the laser beam has to be controlled by an electrical servo system with a high degree of precision since the tracks are very narrow and very close together.

There are believed to be another four or five equally incompatible video disc systems under development.

(b) Film-based systems

Lasers are also used in systems under development which use holograms as part of the recording technique. Holograms are records of interference patterns which are produced when light of one specific frequency (as produced by a laser) overlaps light from the same source which has travelled by a slightly different path. Where the two light waves are in phase, and therefore reinforcing each other, there will be a bright spot and where they are half a wavelength out of phase, and therefore cancelling each other, there will be a dark spot. Such holograms can be recorded on photographic film and reproduced in the form of an embossing on any convenient medium (e.g. cheap plastic tape). The quality of the pictures, reproduced by reading the embossed tape with another laser beam, is virtually unaffected by dust or scratches on the plastic tape.

Any device using photographic film is essentially a replay-only system since the recording itself cannot be erased and reused. However in the case of 8 and 16mm film many users can afford their own cameras to produce software for their projectors.

Broadcasters have long used elaborate telecine machines for converting 35 and 16mm film images into television signals. These either use a combination of film projector and television camera or a special flying-spot tube in which a beam of electrons scans the image thrown on to the face of the tube and, by measuring the intensity of light at each point, directly generates an equivalent television signal.

Several simplified Super-8 telecine devices using one or other of the above techniques have been produced. These are complementary to the use of Super-8 cine film in normal projection equipment, and enable the user to show films on one or more television receivers.

Non-standard high resolution film is the basis of the Electronic Video Reproduction system. In this an electron beam is used to produce a row of monochrome pictures together with variable-density recordings of the colour information and two sound tracks on a fine-grain master film from which the recordings are optically copied. The replay unit has a telecine type scanning unit to produce the required colour television signal.

5. Fascimile recorders

One further type of recorder, viz. that used for facsimile, is of interest, although it cannot produce moving pictures. Current equipment is used for many purposes, e.g. (a) by the press for sending copies of photographs over telephone circuits, a process started some 40 years ago and developed recently to permit similar transmission of complete newspapers; (b) by ships for receiving weather charts by radio; (c) by commercial, insurance, and banking organizations for exchanging financial statements etc., over private wires.

The application of the latest electronic and electro-mechanical technique has made it possible to produce compact economic and efficient desk-top machines for business use which will transmit and receive any written, printed or sketched material. There are many competing recording methods, and future developments involving the combination of xerox and facsimile techniques and the use of solid-state instead of the more expensive electro-mechanical devices are likely to lead to cheaper and more reliable units suitable for domestic use. This may pave the way for electronic mail and newspaper delivery via the telephone network.

In the future, facsimile may develop in quite new directions. For example current experiments using a laser-beam scanner deflected by an acousto-optic device have shown that using this method pictures with three or four times the detail of conventional television can be taken at the sending end and projected at the receiving terminal.

D. COMPUTING AND CONTROL EQUIPMENT

To the casual observer major computer centres may appear to remain very much the same as they were five or ten years before, but in fact comparatively rapid changes are taking place as a result of continuous technological developments. Great increases in total computing capacity, often at reduced cost, are being achieved by changes in each of the components of the computer centre as shown in the diagram below (see figure 2).

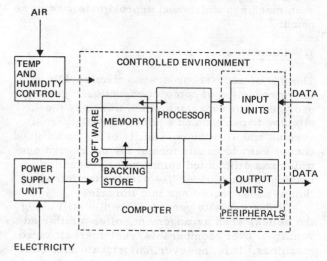

Fig. 2 – A Typical Computer Centre

1. Environmental control

Many computer peripherals still need to work in a temperature and humidity controlled atmosphere. However, the power needed by computers is less, so that smaller supply units can now be used which produce less heat, with the demands on the environmental control plant consequently less severe. (An exception to this trend has been the introduction of a type of memory unit which has needed to employ liquid nitrogen plant in order to permit working at very low temperatures.) However the development of solid-state and possibly magnetic-bubble memory units will remove this particular problem.

2. The processor

The valve-transistor-integrated circuit large-scale integration chain of development of electronic circuit elements has had a very marked affect on computer processors, allowing them to become more sophisticated and develop increased capacity, while at the same time becoming physically smaller.

3. The memory

Computer memory units are still getting smaller and this trend will probably continue longer than in the case of the processors. Large computers are using larger random access memory systems, hence reducing the size of core drums.

They are also using such innovations as hardware paging - a technique whereby parts of the memory are established as separate units or pages with the advantage that access to any part of an individual page can be accelerated.

4. Backing stores

The requirement for ever larger backing stores continues and seems likely to increase for a long while. However this apparently runaway situation is being held in check by improvements in current storage techniques which use some form of magnetic material. These include:

(a) higher packing densities arising from improvements in coding systems and in electro-magnetic recording techniques;

(b) more efficient file handling of software and hardware;

(c) memories divided into modules each using a removable disc.

For the future, storage based on holographic techniques seems to offer tremendous potential.

5. Input and output

As the demand on computer centres increases both in terms of total data to be handled and in range of activities required, so the input and output devices must try to keep in step.

This process is facilitated by:

(a) the development of faster line printers, card readers, etc.;

(b) the use of improved "spooling" techniques which use discs or tapes as buffers, so that input and output devices as well as processors can be kept running as long as possible at maximum speed;

(c) a greater proportion of real-time inquiries which reduce the need for print-outs;

(d) increased real-time data input from remote terminals;

(e) a move away from punched-card readers towards input systems using visual display techniques, magnetic tape or magnetic discs;

(f) developments in optical character recognition which will continue to grow in importance. Improvements are still required to readers capable of providing data input to the computer from hand prepared documents;

(g) the development of techniques for direct output connexions with microfilm production units;

(h) development of computer graphic display devices aided by direct digital input;

(i) the possibility of full-scale computer to computer communication made possible by high speed data communication links between centres;

(j) the development, still at an early stage, of speech recognition systems which will allow man to have voice communication with computers.

The most important needs are improvements in teleprocessing, speed and quality of printers, and large screen graphic display units. The current high cost of the latter two components represents one of the major hurdles in creating widespread individual or small group access to computer networks.

6. Software

Since the introduction of the first computer languages in the mid-1950s the development of software technology has been quite as significant as the parallel hardware development.

Large computers are now only as good as their operating systems, i.e. the programmes which organize the machines' activities in terms of:

(a) resource allocation;

(b) scheduling;

(c) validation;

(d) security;

(e) accounting and billing;

(f) housekeeping;

(g) diagnostic testing.

Part or all of these are held in the memory core all the time. The capacity thus required is therefore considerable, but in a large system it is worthwhile because it results in:

(a) less operator intervention;

(b) better use of the facility, e.g. by having many programmes in the core at once;

(c) more flexibility and control.

In parallel with the development of operating systems, there have been improvements in the use of memories by the development of re-entrant software. This software allows a single copy of a programme to be used by several people at the same time by each user having a unique data area which contains not only his own data but the status of his particular job with respect to the programme.

At the same time language compilers, although getting larger, now generate more efficient machine codes.

These two developments have led to larger systems programmes but greater user efficiency and through-put.

Large systems now have extensive libraries of utility routines for such things as:

(a) file handling;

(b) user error correction and recovery;

(c) text editing;

(d) input/output routines;

(e) scientific sub-routines;

(f) standard package programmes.

7.   Computer trends

Without the hardware and software development described above the provision by computer centres of the many facilities now demanded by users would have required vast machines if they were based on the best technology of the early 1960s.

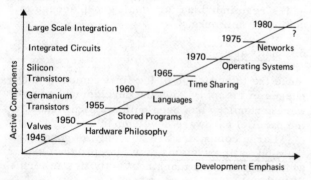

Fig. 3 – The Last 30 Years of Computer Development

At the same time as the development of computer centres and networks there has been another trend favouring the development of small special purpose computers. Such mini computers, as well as being usable independently, can also be used as interconnexions between local terminal units and remote major computers. Terminal units are getting cheaper, yet more versatile and efficient. From large, noisy teleprinter keyboard machines they are moving to compact, silent units which in addition to keyboards may have such facilities as visual display units on which drawings can be produced and modified by interactive light pens.

Although having a different design philosophy, pocket and desk-top calculators which now make use of large-scale integration techniques are reducing rapidly in size, weight and cost while becoming more sophisticated. One machine, for example, now provides slightly improved calculating facilities, yet shows a weight reduction to $\frac{1}{60}$ and cost reduction to $\frac{1}{5}$ of the comparable figures for its predecessor five years earlier. Some designs already include facilities for external connexion to a computer network. At this stage they are virtually indistinguishable from some forms of computer terminals.

Current developments towards computer networks are helped by:

(a) better understanding of input/output procedures;

(b) minicomputers - used as message processors;

(c) communications networks - broadband high speed lines and channels;

(d) software to handle such systems;

(e) a better understanding of the needs of potential users.

The first type of simple network which allowed a number of user terminals to share time on a central computer (see figure 4) is now giving way to distributed computer networks with a few large central processing and information centres (see figure 5).

These networks will tend to become hierarchical leading to a small number of large centres, many intermediate centres and large numbers of small local processing units with many terminal users (c.f. telephone networks).

All nodes of these networks have the common features that they can operate independently and also have the ability to communicate. The trend therefore once again seems to be towards small calculators becoming computers of greater sophistication with built-in telecommunication and storage facilities enabling them to become terminals of large networks when required.

Such units can also be used to control other telecommunication processes, so that when connected to a cable network as well as performing the complex tasks as a computer terminal (e.g. for user participation in some form of computer based learning) they can also carry out the far less demanding tasks of selecting a desired information or television channel and interacting with it. The terminal units of the

Mitre Corporation's TICCIT development may become the first working example of this type of development.

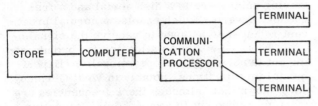

Fig. 4 – Time-Sharing Network

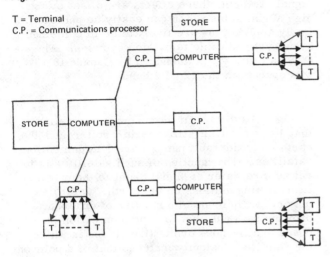

T = Terminal
C.P. = Communications processor

Fig. 5 – Modern Computer Network

E. TRANSMISSION AND DISTRIBUTION EQUIPMENT SYSTEMS

1. Telephone systems

Throughout the world the demands for more telephone services both of existing and new types continue to increase at a pace which is still quickening. To try to meet these demands communication engineers must develop and install:

(a) transmission circuits with wider and wider bandwidths sufficient to accommodate all the signals;

(b) switching and exchange systems able to cope with the increasing number of interconnexions required at a higher speed than before.

They must also carry out these two improvement processes without adversely affecting the vast existing system and at all times ensuring complete compatability with it.

The world-wide telephone network is divisible into four parts, viz. local, junction, trunk and international networks. These all started as analogue systems transmitting speech over pairs of wires in cables and were interconnected by manual switching at exchanges. The vast majority of telephone exchanges in the world now use automatic electro-mechanical switching typified by the Strowger and Crossbar systems (see Chapter 8 - Appendix and technical glossary).

Current developments include:

(a) increasing provision for other services, particularly data transmission;

(b) movement towards semi, and in time fully, electronic exchanges with no moving parts;

(c) the use of frequency-division-multiplexing (FDM) to allow a step-up of the channel carrying capabilities of existing cable networks.

Future developments are planned to provide a universal PCM system based on standards set by the International Telephone and Telegraph Consultative Committee (CCITT). Such digital transmission and switching systems will eventually be able to handle a mixture of all types of signal from stop/start, through data at all levels of quantity and complexity up to broadcast television and including speech, music, facsimile, videophone, confravision, etc.

The bandwidth or bit-rate required for various services is summarized in Table 2 in Chapter 8 - Appendix and technical glossary. The present and proposed development of the four parts of the system are summarized in Table 3.

2. Cable television systems

(a) High frequency (HF) systems. In this system each signal is modulated on to a high frequency carrier which is conveyed to the subscriber via a twisted pair of conductors in a special cable. A separate circuit is provided for each channel or programme. Sound is carried at audio frequencies on the vision circuit and filtered out at the receiver.

Domestic installations of this type are found in a number of cities throughout the world.

(b) HF plus dial access. When the number of channels on an HF system rises above about 15 to 18 it becomes uneconomic to carry every channel to every subscriber. Instead a dial-access system can be used in which each subscriber has only two pairs of wires connected to his outlet. One pair enables him to dial a number to a local programme exchange which connects his selected programme (combined vision and sound) to the second pair of wires which feed his receiver. Exchanges are situated at intervals of one or two miles along the main cable trunk routes. Currently experimental systems of this type have a 36 channel capacity but theoretically there is no upper limit.

(c) Very high frequency (VHF) systems. VHF systems are multi-channel carrier systems using several - a stack of - different carrier frequencies. The signals, up to a normal maximum of nine, are all transmitted together down a single coaxial cable.

3. Radiative systems

(a) <u>Terrestrial</u>. By the use of different types of aerial at the transmitter radio signals can either be beamed in a particular direction or broadcast in all directions. If the carrier frequency is high enough the beam can be made very narrow; it is then of particular value for point-to-point links which are an alternative to the use of cables.

The use of the radio frequency spectrum is governed by international agreement which is regulated by the International Telecommunications Union. Blocks of spectrum space are allocated for specific services which include such things as marine radio communications and radio beacons for guiding ships and aircraft as well as broadcasting and fixed services.

Each country has to decide the purposes to which its allocation of frequencies is put and must then ensure that their use is rigorously controlled. The electromagnetic spectrum is a very important but limited resource on which the demand is constantly growing. A serious challenge is presented to engineers to prevent the complete saturation of the spectrum by reducing the demand from those services where its use is indispensible, and by avoiding its use whenever possible in cases where alternatives can be used.

Because of the comparatively narrow bandwidth required large numbers of sound radio stations can be accommodated on the medium and high frequency bands. However television requires far more bandwidth and even in the VHF part of the spectrum the bands allocated to television permit only a very limited number of transmitters to operate.

The higher the definition of the picture (i.e. the number of lines - 405, 525, 625 or more) the greater will be the bandwidth occupied. Working with low-power transmitters a VHF service can provide several simultaneous programme channels in small areas of high population density so long as no attempt is made to provide a service between such areas. Alternatively working with high power transmitters national coverage is possible but for a strictly limited number of channels.

The UHF part of the spectrum provides more bandwidth and can therefore support more channels but the propagation is more sensitive to terrain contours than VHF and the normal range of reception of 40-60 km. radius around a transmitting station relies on good line-of-sight paths. For 100% coverage of an area many "fill-in" repeater stations may be necessary.

There are more than 100 different networks currently operating in the 2.5-2.69 GHz band in the United States. They provide a 4-channel Instructional Television Fixed Service (ITFS). The transmitter power is regulated, producing a service range of about 30 km. At each receiving point there is a dish aerial and a frequency converter which enables a normal broadcast receiver to be used to receive the signals.

The 12 GHz band is allocated for broadcasting but is not yet in use operationally. Experimental investigations, notably in West Germany, have shown that, although these frequencies are much more subject to atmospheric attenuation and heavy rain can cause a considerable drop in signal strength, these effects are offset by the high aerial gains which can easily be achieved. Early applications are likely to be in combined broadcast and cable television systems. The CTS satellite, to be launched by Canada in 1975, will operate in the 12 GHz band.

(b) <u>Satellite</u>. Of the man-made satellites that have been or still are in orbit round the earth a considerable number are communications satellites. The function of such satellites is to act as a repeater of signals sent to them from transmitting stations on the earth. Satellites may be put into one of a number of different orbiting patterns, but for communication purposes synchronous orbits (i.e. those in which the satellite's velocity matches that of a point on the earth's equator and the satellite remains at a height of approximately 22,300 miles above it) are generally the most advantageous, although the USSR gains from using an elliptical non-synchronous orbit because of that country's particular location on the earth's surface.

A communication satellite therefore requires positioning and orientation controls and a telemetry system which provides position information to the earth and responds to command signals from the earth. It also requires receiving and transmitting aerials and the receiver/amplifier/transmitter which forms the repeater. To drive this it needs electrical energy produced by the solar panels which form its "battery".

Communications satellites can be either:

(a) point-to-point - using relatively low-powered satellites with large and expensive earth stations. Suitable for data, telephone and television signal links between widely separated countries that have well developed internal communication networks; or

(b) distribution - using medium-powered satellites providing a fairly strong signal over a limited area within which reception is possible by earth stations costing about $100,000 from which distribution by rebroadcasting to a limited area would be possible. Such systems are in use in the USSR and Canada and under active consideration in a number of other countries; or

(c) broadcasting - using a high-powered satellite providing a strong signal, over a wide area, which can be received by inexpensive earth terminals located at community viewing centres. Such a system is possible now but increasing the power of the satellite to a level sufficient to relay a television signal directly to an individual home receiver is beyond the capabilities of satellites existing or planned for the next decade.

Distribution type satellites may, as in Canada now, make access to television programmes produced at some distant centre an added attraction to individuals connected to a local cable network. However, it is the broadcast satellite which has the potential to give direct access to information to millions of people in both developed and developing countries. If current trends continue it will eventually be possible to use cheap terminal receivers for data, computer links, radio and television.

CHAPTER 6

The next ten years and beyond

It goes without saying that not everything which is feasible, or which has been described in the previous chapter, will actually come to pass. Our technological capacity is always in advance of performance, governed by the limitations already described in Chapter 2. In making general forecasts, therefore, we have to match capacity to the prevailing environment, taking account of both favourable and unfavourable aspects.

No attempt can be made here to analyse social, political or economic limitations, although these will inevitably have a marked impact on development. A number of such factors are likely to encourage, or retard, development: for example, copyright restrictions, legal and statutory controls on transmission or frequency allocation, commercial and marketing considerations (which can often work against the present tendency in education and communication towards greater individualization). Many of the parameters controlling development are associated with the production of software, and it is always salutary to remind ourselves that, whatever technological solutions are available or chosen, the costs and problems of producing relevant software will always be greater, in the long run, than for hardware.

However, this admission does leave us in some difficulty, precisely because the future does depend largely upon non-technical factors. In particular it depends upon decisions, by administrations, manufacturers and governments, as to how they are going to use technology.

In the end, there are two kinds of future. There is a random future, in which development proceeds from normal social, political and commercial exchanges - on the level of commitment to existing technology (and hence its perpetuation), on mass production and distribution experiences, on social pressures and influences. There is also a more disciplined future, in which a systems

approach to planning, at all levels, matches medium and technology to function, and in which the design of equipment and of software are allowed to interact. The prospects for the next decade are poised between these two alternatives.

Accordingly, the chapter which follows is only an informed guess, based on an extrapolation of trends. It takes account of current enthusiasms, economic conditions, areas of rapid development, and it identifies in particular those technologies which are unlikely to move forward with any rapidity. In a final chapter, the position of the developing world will be looked at more critically, and the prospects of alternative or intermediate technologies considered - which do depend upon a deliberate decision to subordinate means to needs.

A. GENERAL

The most significant development in the field of electronics has been the evolution of large-scale integration techniques. Any equipment such as the parts of a computer or television network which makes use of them can easily be made both more sophisticated and cheaper.

Transistor radios are now bringing a form of aural "literacy" to millions of people in developing countries. The costs of programme production, transmission and reception are all very low compared with television via satellites, terrestrial transmitters or cables. Using television means that, in order to justify the high transmission and reception costs, a large number of programmes must be produced. Although the production costs of these may be anywhere between $1,300 per hour quoted for educational television production in El Salvador and the hourly production rate of $48,000 for the American pre-school programme "Sesame Street" it is certain that they will far exceed those of comparable radio programmes. But the big step from radio to television appears to go unchallenged in most countries with no more real justification than the historical fact that television was invented soon after radio.

With the development of LSI and solid-state display matrices, it would only require a suitable delay-line to make possible the mass production of a portable battery driven radio receiver which could also display still pictures. It would appear to have much greater potential than either slide-tape or radio-vision techniques.

In developed countries where the introduction of extensive multi-channel cable systems is feasible the critical factor is likely to be the development of a really cheap multipurpose terminal unit which will allow a range of different signals - television, data, facsimile, etc. - to be received and a more restricted range of responses to be made. LSI will make a significant contribution to reducing the cost of such terminal units but an equally important contribution will only be forthcoming if the reliance on moving parts can be reduced or removed altogether. Equipment with such parts is relatively more expensive to produce and also to maintain, since its reliability will inevitably be lower than that of solid state electronic equipment. In a few years' time the historical significance of the PLATO project may well prove to be in the particular type of terminal that was developed to achieve this objective. The recognition of the need to use a digital type display system in which there were no moving parts - not even an electron beam - led to the use of the plasma panel with its thousands of digitally addressable points.

B. CHANNEL SPACE

The electromagnetic spectrum is an inelastic resource. The higher frequencies, while offering more information-carrying bandwidth, at the same time offer smaller area-covering-potential unless a satellite transmitter is used. It seems likely therefore that until such time as very large satellites, capable of carrying powerful transmitters, are in general use for broadcasting, as distinct from relaying programmes, other means will have to be found for effectively increasing channel space. Satellites of the required proportions are not planned for the next ten years and it will probably be at least a further ten years before they are widely available. They are therefore unlikely to make any great impact on the world's educational problems in the next decade. Apart from one or two educational experiments it is not likely to be until after major commercial interests in telephone, data and other links have been satisfied that any permanent

broadcasting by satellite will be established. However, demand for increased choice of channels to meet individual requirements rather than those of the masses continues to grow.

We can therefore recognize pressures to restrict the use of frequency space to those services which must use it, thereby limiting the frequencies available for broadcasting. At the same time conflicting pressures to provide more channel space are becoming apparent. This must result in (a) moves to take up the slack and utilize the latent potential of existing transmitters, e.g. by 24 hour services with some automatic recording at reception points; (b) increasing use of cable systems for television leading in perhaps 20 years to compulsory restriction of many services in densely populated areas to this means of transmission; (c) increasing use of pre-recorded material in a number of formats for those with specialist interests.

Further exploitation of telephone networks is possible in most countries, but the problems vary with the existing state of development. The following analysis of the United Kingdom situation serves to illustrate the type of difficulties which are likely to arise:

(a) Strowger type electro-mechanical exchange facilities are still being expanded to keep pace with increasing demand for phones;

(b) push-button dialling systems - essential for many feedback systems - are pointless with the existing Strowger exchanges and therefore are not yet being encouraged;

(c) there is a big clamour for more phones, but when people have them they make relatively little use of them. The network is only 1% used in terms of time and capacity;

(d) those with phones appear quite interested in the services offered which include the speaking clock, weather forecasts, test match scores for cricket enthusiasts, dial-a-disc for pop fans, recipes for the housewife, etc. In 1971-1972, 434 million such calls brought the Post Office of £4.3 million in revenue;

(e) the proposed very wideband trunk circuits have not yet been operated even experimentally;

(f) if they prove successful they will cut the cost per circuit but only if there is extensive use of the bandwidth which they will make available;

(g) such extensive use must assume a big demand for viewphones, confravision, and multichannel television;

(h) if in time a demand develops there will still be a marketing (or moral) problem. Can one install viewphones each of which occupies the band space of 250 telephones, when there is a waiting list for telephones?

(i) there is as yet very little evidence to suggest that there will be sufficient public support to justify the general introduction of viewphones since commercial organizations which would be best able to afford the service and which also have most to gain by savings in time and travelling expenses of busy executives show few signs of wanting such a service;

(j) less than 1% of the junction networks are of the digital - PCM type. The rate of installation of digital equipment is barely keeping pace with the rate of total expansion in response to demands for new telephones;

(k) at the present rate it will be ten years before the last analogue facilities are ordered for the trunk circuits and therefore many years more before existing equipment can be replaced.

Hence it seems reasonable to conclude that during the next decade there will be:

(a) a growth in the existing type of phone services;

(b) a development at unequal rates of trunk, junction and local wideband networks;

(c) an increase in data and computer services;

(d) very little development of the use of the viewphone.

The possibility of developing a national-coverage wired distribution system will depend upon having a high potential utilization factor which in turn means that a variety of services including television must be offered. Such facilities would require a coaxial cable local network together with very wideband and therefore digital type junction and trunk networks. Such a project would cost about £1,000 million at current prices. By the time that there is a sufficiently bouyant economy for such a project to be seriously considered the costs will have risen several times. It therefore appears very unlikely to be started in the next ten years despite the fact that the technical know-how exists. If the country did not have such a high level of capital investment in the existing system, if it were a developing country with only an elementary telephone network, then a universal wideband system with potential for many different applications could be installed and progressively developed over a number of years.

C.   FEEDBACK

Technical developments have already made live phone-in and on-the-spot audio and video contributions via radio links an accepted part of normal broadcasting. However, under the control of professional broadcasters who for a variety of reasons are always concerned to maximize their audience, they will probably stabilize at somewhere between 5 and 15% of the stations' output depending on their popularity with the listeners and viewers.

Logically all new cable systems should have

some means of data feedback incorporated in their design. This would ensure that the line amplifiers, unlike those in the majority of existing networks, would be capable of handling feedback signals. The two most important uses of data feedback in cable systems will be first, the provision of an opportunity for the subscriber to select from an increasing number of programme or information channels, and second, the provision of a means whereby the subscriber may respond to questions or requests presented to him on his television screen.

After initial field trials in the next few years it seems likely that television receivers might include, as a small additional unit, a data control and feedback device, which would enable the television set to be used to receive data sent as part of a broadcast signal, over a cable network or via the telephone system. In the latter two cases it could provide the user with a means of responding.

D.   PRODUCTION AND RECORDING EQUIPMENT

The trend here is clearly towards simpler to operate but higher quality equipment at lower cost. This is particularly true of equipment which is not intended for use by professional broadcasters. In order to ensure complete technical acceptability of material made by access groups there is still a need for a number of improvements in most portable videotape recorders if they are to be stable enough to be used to drive cable or broadcasting systems without additional equipment. The sound quality on most portable machines could also be improved.

Digital circuit techniques, which by their fundamental nature are more suitable for the mass replication techniques associated with large-scale integration, are already being applied wherever possible in the development of new television production, control and recording equipment. By the end of the decade there should be some experimental television systems in operation which are completely digital from the light input point to the light output point. When such systems have been properly developed a new era of picture information handling will begin in which a complete range of sophistication or picture quality will become available. This will be very similar to the present state of electronic calculators, in which by paying a little more for additional digital circuits the customer has the option of buying a machine which gives answers to a few more decimal places.

Another important development during the next ten years is likely to be a rapid spread of video cassette recording. It will be interesting to see whether video discs, coming in the wake of tape cassettes, will ever achieve the premier position that audio discs held when they were first in the field. The price of discs could be a lot less than that of tapes but in practice it is usually the programme material that determines the major part of the cost.

Some fairly rapid changes can also be expected in facsimile techniques. Over the last decade facsimile has changed very little except for the reduction in transmission times. Most transmissions are still via radio links or private telephone lines. There are many potential applications of facsimile but those organizations which might have adopted it have been slow to do so for one or more of the following reasons:

(a) the incompatibility between machines of different manufacturers;

(b) the quality of the copy produced;

(c) the relatively slow transmission time which is normally six minutes for an A4 size document when sent over the public telephone system. (This time compares favourably with Telex, which requires nine minutes to transmit a full 60-line page of 600 words.)

If, as seems likely, these problems are overcome during the next ten years, a large growth in the use of facsimile can be expected, and in particular a move to make greater use of public telephone networks for transmission. If this occurs the idea of an "electronic mail" service might become a reality and start to reduce the load on increasingly expensive postal services. It would also have the effect of moving facsimile apparatus out of the high quality but very costly hand-built equipment bracket into the cheaper mass-produced range. It could then become available for domestic use in conjunction with cable or broadcast television systems.

The incompatibility problem is still a major concern. However, it is possible that a "fall-back" mode of operation may soon be standardized. The "fall-back" mode although slower would allow inter-machine operation between all systems. This would not restrict higher speed operation between machines of an individual manufacturer.

Quality is directly related to the bandwidth of the transmission channel and the time taken for transmission. When considering the use of the public telephone system the bandwidth is automatically limited, therefore any increase in quality or speed can only be achieved by some form of information compression. Several are available but all increase the complexity and cost of the equipment required.

E. THE GROWING INFLUENCE OF THE COMPUTER

It is certain that computers will have a major influence both on the media themselves and on all types of access to them. The big will grow bigger - vast computer data banks containing programmes and information on every field of human interest will be built up over the next two or three decades. Many of these will be shared internationally via satellite and thus be of immense value to developing nations. At the same time, the small will get even smaller - the computer terminal unit - the man-machine interface - benefiting from LSI, will reduce in size, weight, energy consumption and cost. This could also become apparent within the next decade. If a sufficiently bold approach is made, a multipurpose unit could be standardized which could be used:

(a) independently for calculations;

(b) connected to a television receiver for visual display;

(c) if the receiver is fed from a suitable cable system, for data display and interaction;

(d) connected to the telephone network for access to large computers for all types of data including that providing a facsimile type print out.

Computer circuit elements are being developed more quickly and their cost is falling more rapidly than those of any other field of electronics. They will therefore continue to be adopted or adapted for any other area of telecommunications where they can be used.

Computers are being used increasingly in the management of complex processes and systems. Starting with essential areas such as nuclear power stations and some chemical processing plant, then moving on to lower priority areas such as stock control and banking, the developments have now reached areas such as the management of learning and of telephone network switching. Development in these latter areas will continue, but here too by the end of another decade computer aided management will be considered essential rather than desirable in all forward planning.

There will be a need to train both existing and future generations in the use of computer terminals. The intensive work at present under way in many centres will produce programming improvements which will make it virtually unnecessary for the ordinary user to know what happens on the computer network to which his own small terminal is connected.

The United Kingdom's Open University will be offering a course in 1975 for which each student will receive a mini-computer on loan. This is being done because it should prove more economical than providing the essential computing practice on the terminals of a larger network which the university already has available in many colleges. While this is only a half step forward in terms of the forecasts made earlier in this section it is an example of giving older students first-hand experience of computer operation and at the same time reflects the falling costs resulting from the micro-electronic circuit developments.

F. STORAGE AND RETRIEVAL

In 1969 after an extensive study of educational technology in the United States, Richard Hooper wrote: "A major complaint, especially from teachers, about the newer media centres is the question of accessibility. Given the existence of good materials, can they be got at and used? ... The media people themselves suffer from these problems of accessibility. The task of locating materials from catalogues and brochures is formidable. Book libraries have been around for hundreds of years and many people still do not know how to use them and are apprehensive of cataloguing systems. Film clips, still pictures, discs and tapes, lie in their millions across the country, unknown, often uncatalogued, and mostly unused. Once located, the problems of retrieval and evaluation are, despite the growth of video-tape, audio-tape and film libraries, vast."(1)

The position in the United States and elsewhere has not changed radically in the last five years as far as the ordinary teacher or student is concerned. However, a lot of research and development work and numerous field trials are under way with the object of improving the storage and retrieval of all types of information in many different formats.

Once stored, both book and non-book materials have to be catalogued. Unfortunately, information is put into catalogues in many different ways. If more compatible methods could be devised this would greatly assist international transfer of information.

The problem of non-browsable material has been mentioned on a number of occasions, and presents an important challenge to technologists. If all types of material could be easily and quickly browsed, the effective use of media in all levels of education would be greatly stimulated. Words are not really an adequate summary of the visual contents of a film or television programme but a careful selection of shots might be strung together to make an informative rather than a stimulative type of "trailer". An even better method, if it could be achieved, would be for the potential user to be able to scan very rapidly through the programme seeing and hearing clearly but at a variable speed which he could control.

The average person speaks at a rate of about 150 words per minute, but people have been trained to speak at rates as fast as 300 words per minute and it is quite easy to listen and comprehend speech at this rate. Electronic equipment exists which can compress recorded speech, by shortening pauses and vowel sounds. Such devices, which will fall in price with electronic circuit improvements, offer considerable potential for reducing the time needed to listen to a lecture. It would also make audio-journalism more competitive time-wise with the printed page.

(1) R. Hooper: "Diagnosis of Failure", AV Communication Review, Vol. 17, No. 3, 1969.

CHAPTER 7

Systems planning and low-cost technologies

Access to educational materials, and life-long education in some form, must become both the need and the right of virtually the whole population in both developed and developing countries. As this altruistic target is progressively accepted throughout the world, because of the growing numbers involved there will always be severe financial constraints on the process of providing access to learning opportunities. Even limited success cannot be achieved without careful planning, including consideration of the efficiency and effectiveness of any new technology which might be introduced.

A. SYSTEMS ANALYSIS

There are a number of benefits to be gained from applying a systems approach to their problem, since the solutions in almost every case will be a judicious mixture of methods and means. The use of the correct mix will lead to improved efficiency and hence greater economy. A systems approach will also assist in the process of discovering the critical path in an actual or desired development programme.

In any unit of the total system which is proposing to make use of modern media, a careful study of the working environment is the first step. This should always be followed by defining accurately the particular social and educational objectives. Then planning should proceed to identify appropriate methods and media. Starting from the media which have the lowest information level, tests should be conducted to determine the necessary level of complexity required to achieve the objectives. In many cases an a acceptable and much cheaper solution may be found than that likely to be proposed by equipment salesmen or others with vested interests. The system, if it is to be and to remain efficient, must have arrangements for assessment and

adequate feedback incorporated in its design. In practice it will be found that any existing system (mechanical, institutional or human) has considerable inertia - a quality which helps to protect it from violent disturbances, revolutionary ideas or extremists but also a quality which tends to inhibit desirable developments. It is therefore very important for those who wish to bring about changes in any existing system to be able to identify the true nature of its inertia. For example, analysis may reveal that the true brake on new developments is the existing level of capital investment rather than technical difficulties.

This has certainly been the case, for example, in the field of video recording for broadcast television where, for nearly a decade, the vast investment in very expensive video recorders with four rotating heads moving across 2-inch wide magnetic tape has led to an ever increasing committal to this format despite the competing claims of other types of machine. A similar study of existing communication transmission or distribution methods in a country may reveal comparable problems due to existing levels of capital investment.

The rapid growth of complex computer controlled systems has led to the emergence of a new type of engineer who is concerned with the architecture of the total system rather than the individual components or sub-systems. If past mistakes, arising from the haphazard patchwork of systems, are not to be repeated, the planning of total systems should be given pride of place over the concurrent development of materials, processes, hardware and software. This principle appears to be equally applicable to both telecommunication and educational systems.

B. THE IMPLICATIONS OF SYSTEMS

Techniques of systems analysis may be especially

relevant in the developing world, where low-cost, high-yield solutions have to be found. Finding the appropriate technology does not merely mean accepting simple rather than complex systems or devices; for there are a whole lot of social, psychological and economic factors that have to be taken into account if innovations are to be successful. In developing countries, particularly, great care is needed in the introduction of patterns of technological development that may make a real contribution towards relieving unemployment and the social frustrations which stem from poverty and inadequate basic amenities.

A systems analysis may show that the appropriate technological solution for educational development is any one of a range of different possibilities, e.g.:

(a) riding pick-a-back on some general commercial development intended for widespread domestic or entertainment markets;

(b) being courageous enough to make a large and expensive central investment which will lead to very low costs for large numbers of users;

(c) using some form of intermediate technology which profits from a particular environment and helps the producing community in other ways;

(d) assessing the minimum essential level of information which may lead to the adoption of a specific low-cost technology. Some of these, such as slow-scan television, may be technically attractive (e.g. when only narrow bandwidth communication channels are available), but may be less acceptable from a psychological viewpoint. Others such as the audio cassette, which is also an example of a pick-a-back development, are proving their acceptability.

C. TECHNOLOGY AND THE REDUCTION OF COSTS

Technology is a means of lowering cost in many situations, but only when intelligently applied. The appropriate means will only be thrown up by coherent analysis, but the following are some characteristic solutions.

1. Introduction of a new system

Probably one of the best examples of a new system being introduced rather than a repetition of a known and tried system is that of the Open University in the United Kingdom. The University provides degree and post-experience courses for working adults to graduate and post-graduate levels by a combination of correspondence teaching, television and radio programmes and face-to-face tuition. The University is organized into six faculties, a regional tutorial service (with 13 regions) and an Institute of Educational Technology.

Students (45,000 in 1973) obtain their degrees by completing a set number of credits.

Although initial expenditure on the establishment of the Open University was high, the scale on which the system was implemented has proved its worth, and the methods employed are showing themselves to be more economical than the usual high costs of university teaching, with savings being made especially on building costs.

2. More economic ways of using existing systems

In many countries sophisticated video distribution systems exist which are grossly underutilized. With the advent of new recording techniques the spare capacity of night hours could be taken up on broadcast networks.

Extra use can be made of existing facilities following certain technical developments. A description has already been given of the systems being developed which make use of the "gaps" in the television signal. With the addition of a small unit to the receiver the viewer can obtain various items of information from his domestic television receiver, giving him a different supplementary use from his equipment at a reasonable cost.

The telephone networks which are in operation are in most cases underused. However, telephone lines can now be used for other purposes.

Devices such as the "Electrowriter" provide examples of means of transmitting information along ordinary telephone lines. Two electronic "pens" are linked along the lines. At the transmission end the teacher writes or draws on a continuous roll of acetate film on the receiver. This receiver has a built-in overhead projector which projects the writings, diagrams, etc., on to a screen.

3. Cheap machines and materials

The costs of many items of equipment are now being dramatically reduced. The compact cassette, for example, has had a revolutionary effect on audio recording. Mass production meant that the machines fell in price and immediately the demand rose, the cassettes themselves are cheap and can be copied in bulk. Any item which can be mass produced in this way will force prices down. The advent of the video disc will, probably in the domestic market initially, mean that use of the disc will be widespread and the mass production techniques of pressing out the discs will give cheap and easily replaceable software.

4. Lower information level techniques

Many instances can be found of expensive

technologies being introduced without a thorough cost-effectiveness exercise being done. Moving pictures are usually chosen, distributed by film or television with no real justification being made for their use. Systems such as the integration of radio and slides or still pictures, or tape/slide sequences can often achieve the same ends at a fraction of the cost.

In closed-circuit television systems costs are high mainly because of the cost of the cable or microwave facilities. If continuous motion of pictures is unnecessary, slow-scan television can be used. In this system normal television techniques are used with one exception – the optical image produced in the television camera is scanned comparatively slowly by the electron beam which converts it into an electrical signal. A slow-scan video converter can reduce the bandwidth of the video signal to as little as 1/10,000th of the original. Thus normal telephone lines can be used for transmission. At the receiving end the signal is reconverted for viewing on a conventional television screen by storing the information as it arrives until a complete frame or single picture has been received. One picture can be transmitted in 40 to 50 seconds. If motion is involved pictures showing stages of development at 40 second intervals can be transmitted. Slow-scan television has obvious applications for education when still pictures, graphs, charts, diagrams, photographs etc., are required rather than moving pictures.

5. Savings on professional staff costs

One of the problems facing most countries is the shortage of trained professional staff - both academic and technical. New distribution methods are now enabling information to be transmitted without the intervention of staff.

Self-learning packages are increasingly being developed for use both within educational institutions and for self-improvement courses. No recourse to teachers or professional assistance is usually necessary.

Remote lectures are now taking place using phones or radio, and devices such as the "blackboard-by-wire" system which uses ordinary telephone lines to transmit from an electronic stylus generating signals corresponding to its position in a frame and presenting this on local and remote television monitors.

6. Home-made materials

The production of both hardware and software is often becoming a local industry, bringing employment to previously deprived areas. The materials are produced using locally available resources and the end products are more suited to the needs of their users than more expensive imported materials. Costs can be kept low in any type of institution if materials are made in-house. In every school examples are found of cheaply produced software often specifically geared to the teacher and pupil's own particular needs. Home production is time consuming, but in other ways costs far less than sophisticated commercially produced materials. Software if often produced from cheap, throw-away materials, imaginatively used to produce ideal teaching or learning materials.

D. INTERMEDIATE TECHNOLOGY

The process of communication need not therefore necessarily involve sophisticated and expensive media. Technologically sophisticated solutions have been imposed on a variety of situations which were not ready to accept them and indeed, did not need them. Moving pictures plus sound are often employed at high cost when still pictures or sound alone could have brought equally successful or even better results.

Expenditure per head in most industrialized countries on the capital plant for any new technology is 10 to 30 times as high as in developing countries. Although the number of wage-earning workers in a developing country is likely to be increasing some six times as fast as in an already industrialized country, the costs of new technologies are such that only one-tenth of the population can benefit from them. The obvious outcome of this is that the so-called "dualism" of development occurs - one-tenth of the people becoming richer and living better lives, while the rest remain in the poverty which existed before the introduction of the technology.

Some Western countries have for many decades been working on the principle that whatever is newest and biggest and therefore most costly, is best, yet in many instances where a new technology has been introduced it has been proved that small-scale units can be equally as efficient and effective. The markets in developing countries are often too small to accept large modern units. Factories have been built which are only 14% used; video distribution systems have been installed at high cost when duplicated sheets would have sufficed.

The sophisticated plant of the West results in elaborate products which are often inappropriate to the developing countries. Similarly, production techniques (e.g. in television programmes) may reach too high a level of professionalism for the village audience and be incomprehensible to all but the 10% privileged élite.

Western technologies have been designed to meet Western needs using Western resources.

These are often resources which are not available in the developing country and have to be imported - again at a high cost. Even a simple process like paper production is difficult in a developing country as until recently paper could only be produced from conifers - a resource which is not available in most developing countries.

It has been estimated that 20% of the price which a nation pays for the privilege of having a new technology covers the cost of the research and development which has gone into the technology. The high cost of paying for this knowledge is one which many developing countries are beginning to regard as unnecessary.

Consequently, even while States become independent in a political sense, there are many arguments put forward that the only real independence is technological independence. The rôle of recipient is often seen as that of dependent, that of benefactor becomes imperialist. It is perhaps this argument, closely allied to the economic situation in developing countries, that is the main reason for the move towards what has come to be known as intermediate technology.

The concept of intermediate technology was applied originally to the industrial structures of developing countries, and it is only recently that thought has been given to its application in communication environments. It is, in many ways, an offshoot of systems analysis, in that it depends, initially, upon a close analysis of needs and objectives. But once this is done, and objectives are clearly specified, these are not simply matched to existing media or resources, but the actual technology available is scrutinized, to see how it may be most closely matched to the problems, taking account of such factors as manpower production levels, manufacturing capacity, etc. In this way, capital costs may be lowered, human resources optimized, small-scale units manufacturing appropriate products introduced - and most important, independence in a political, economic and technological sense may be achieved.

The implications of introducing the techniques of intermediate technology into a developing country are deep and wide-ranging. There has to be a conscious move on the part of the government away from the unequal distribution of wealth amongst the one-tenth of the population reached by the advanced technology and its benefits to a genuine desire to see wealth evenly spread. Many experts would claim that it is in China that the true examples of intermediate technology can be found - a state in which the continuing cultural revolution leaves no place for a 10% élite.

It is said that there is a radio in every village of the world - yet grandiose experiments using television via satellites and elaborate video distribution systems are being planned, where in some cases duplicated picture books linked to radio programmes would probably be as effective. Some attempts to reduce the implementation costs of sophisticated technologies are being made (for example, India is producing aerials for group reception of satellite signals from chicken wire for only $30). But the basic concept that a sophisticated satellite technology is necessary has been accepted. Little evaluation has been done of the long standing use of correspondence courses linked to radio, as used in remote parts of Australia, or even radio courses with meeting places established for correction of work if no mail service exists.

Little systematic exploration of the uses to which intermediate technology might be put has been done. The few sporadic examples which have occurred have seldom been adequately monitored or evaluated. Organizations such as Unesco are now setting up studies to look at, for example, microteaching without the use of CCTV in Israel, programmed learning in group meetings in India or the different uses and combinations of radio, often discovering that the introduction of the concept behind the method eliminates the need for the concomitant hardware.

Intermediate technology concepts are being used not only in developing countries but also as self-instructional packaged material for learning both in and out of the institutionalized education system in developed countries. Radiovision - (the use of radio programmes plus slides) and tape/slide sequences are being used in many educational establishments. In the United Kingdom for example, university departments are producing their own courses of individualized instruction for various purposes such as bridging the gap between school and first year university work, for teaching techniques dealing with the acquisition of essential skills or for key topics which can occur at any stage of a course.

E. CONCLUSION

This final chapter has departed somewhat from the rest of this report, in that it has been concerned more with conditions for applying technology. In the developing countries, where basic problems are more considerable, the need for radical solutions, which ignore factors of status and expediency, is at its greatest. But at all levels, the future of communications technology, over the next decade or over the next century, is dependent ultimately, not upon technical invention, but upon its subordination to needs and objectives. Without a proper function, a declared purpose, and without relevant materials to distribute, technology is no more than a device. Access to communications media is important, but it is not an end in itself.

CHAPTER 8

Appendix and technical glossary

Alpha-numeric - code or information containing both letters and numbers.

Amplifier - an electronic device which amplifies any type of electrical signal which is applied to its input.

Attenuation - a reduction in the voltage or power of an electrical signal or wave caused for example by energy losses as the wave moves along a cable.

Back projection - an arrangement which allows a picture to be viewed on a translucent screen from the side opposite to the projector.

Bandwidth - the width of the band of the electromagnetic spectrum occupied by a telecommunication channel.

CARRIER

| LOWER SIDE—BAND | UPPER SIDE-BAND |

Frequency

Bandwidth
A Double-Side-Band System

CARRIER

| LOWER SIDE—BAND |

Frequency

Bandwidth
A Single-Side-Band System

Bit - the smallest unit of information; a binary digit.

Cable television - summary of domestic cable developments: see Table 1.

CAL - computer aided learning.

CATV - community aerial television.

CCTV - closed-circuit television - a system in which reception is restricted to individuals or institutions participating in the activities of a privately owned and operated transmission system.

Coaxial cable - a cable in which the coaxial outer sheath and the central coil are both electrical conductors. They are separated from each other by a suitable insulating material.

Crossbar - a type of telephone exchange in which links are established by way of a matrix of interconnexions.

Dial-access - see page 25.

Double-side-band - see bandwidth.

Efficiency - see page 20.

EVR - electronic video reproduction - see page 33.

Facsimile - see page 34.

Frequency - number of complete waves or cycles per second.

FDM - frequency division multiplexing - a technique which enables a number of separate signals to be superimposed on a single communication channel by frequency sharing.

GHz - gigahertz - 1,000,000,000 Hz.

Hz - hertz - the units in which frequency is measured. 1 hertz = 1 cycle per second.

Hardware - the machines or equipment, large or small, which make up any system. The term is used to distinguish the machines from the materials they use or play (their software).

Helical scan - one type of video tape recorder, see page 33.

Holography - see page 34.

LSI - large-scale integration - see page 29.

Laser - see page 31.

Light pen - a device whose position can be determined by a computer when it is touched on the surface of a VDU. It is thus able to provide an input to a computer which either indicates a selection from choices presented on the screen or indicates a location in terms of cartesian (x, y) co-ordinates where something should happen.

Low-loss liquid - a liquid which does not absorb very much energy from a light wave which passes through.

MARC - machine readable catalogue - see page 27.

MHz - megahertz - 1,000,000 hertz.

Microfilm - a very fine grain photographic film on which printed and other materials are recorded. To read the film a magnifying or projection device is required.

Microform - the collective term for microcard, microfiche, microfilm and any similar recording system which produces a very reduced reproduction of the original.

Microwave - term applied to the very short electromagnetic waves with wavelengths ranging between 1 and 100 cm. These are also known as super high frequency waves with frequencies ranging between 3 and 30 GHz.

Noise - see page 21.

ORACLE - see page 32.

OHP - overhead projector.

Pay t.v. - the name of the company operating a closed circuit television service to private subscribers and offering them programmes additional to those provided by the broadcasters. Now used more generally to describe this type of operation.

Photo-transistor - a transistor which either converts light energy into electrical energy or vice versa.

PLATO - the system is shown in schematic form in figure 1.

The input controller scans all incoming lines from the network for incoming data. A site address is attached to the data, a parity check performed and the information passes on to the computer. At present a total of 1,024 terminals can be serviced by the input controller.

The output controller accepts data from the computer and prepares it for transmission over the network. The data is delivered to the digital television transmitter where it is encoded into a form compatible with the requirements of standard commercial television equipment. The data is sent to television transmitting equipment for modulation and transmission via a video cable.

Most terminals in the system are grouped into sites of up to 32 terminals. The sites each contain a site controller consisting of a digital television receiver and distributor and a line concentrator. The receiver recovers the data from the television channel and distributes it to the terminals over twisted pair lines. The line concentrator transmits data from up to 32 terminals to the computer centre on a single voice grade telephone line.

The PLATO network can also provide services to individual remotely located terminals. Data for these terminals is transmitted over voice grade phones which are connected to a PLATO site controller. This controller is identical to that used in the classroom sites and can be located anywhere in the PLATO network.

Portapak - the trade name of one particular portable television camera and one half inch video

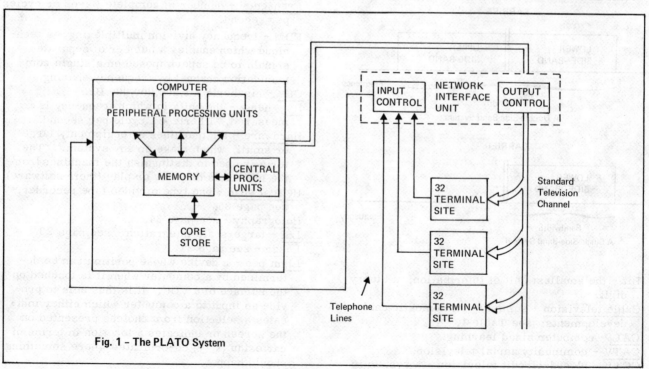

Fig. 1 - The PLATO System

tape recorder unit but often used to describe any such battery operated portable unit.

PCM - pulse code modulation - see page 30.

Radiovision - a technique, pioneered by the BBC, in which radio broadcasts are accompanied by filmstrips.

Random access - a process which allows information to be put into storage or removed from it in such a way that the access time is independent of the particular item and the time or sequence of its storing.

Reliability - the long-term dependability of equipment in service - a quantity which can now be determined more scientifically and with greater accuracy than previously.

Single-side-band - see bandwidth.

Slow-scan television - see page 48.

Software - recorded information in the form of messages or programmes which can be used on one of the many different types of equipment (hardware). Examples of software include computer programmes, television or film programmes, audio or visual material on tapes, slides, transparencies, etc.

Solid-state - see page 31.

Strowger - a type of electro-mechanical telephone exchange invented by a Kansas undertaker named Strowger in 1889. It consists of banks of rotary switches connected in series which means that each switch must rotate to the selected position (1 out of 10) before the next switch can move to its position and so on.

Telecine - see page 34.

Telephone networks - Table 2 (see page 53). shows the bandwidth or bit-rate required for a number of different types of service which the telephone network could carry.
Table 3 (see page 54) summarizes the present and proposed development of the four parts of the telephone system.

Teletype terminal or teleprinter - an electromechanical typewriter that can both transmit and receive messages coded into electrical signals. Used for passing data over radio or telephone networks and between human operators and computers.

Thermionic valve - or radio valve - a vacuum tube device in which electrons are produced from a cathode by thermionic (heat) emission and collected by an anode held at a high voltage which attracts them. This simple two-electrode (or diode) arrangement can be refined by the addition of further electrodes (in the form of grids through which the electrons can pass) which control the electron stream and allow the valve to be used as an amplifier.

TICCIT - a computer based information retrieval system in which each home is connected by cable to central computer and data banks. The subscriber's home terminal equipment includes

a set top converter which must possess the very high channel selectivity required for adjacent channel operation on a VHF stacked-carrier system when this deals with nearly thirty channels in the band 60-300 MHz. For dealing with the two-way facilities proposed for the Washington network two coaxial cables will be required and each terminal unit will also have modulating and demodulating facilities and
(a) a frame snatcher;
(b) an unscrambler;
(c) print-out devices.

In operation the TICCIT computer will address sequential frames of alpha-numeric information to particular subscribers: a group of 3,000 subscribers could have this information up-dated or refreshed every two minutes for every allocated television channel. The unscrambler unit is intended to provide security either for the subscriber when he calls for private data, i.e. bank statements or for the programme originator when transmitting pay television signals. The print-out device can include facsimile or other forms of hard copy.

The Washington Cable Television design includes a tree system of telecasting and several point-to-point links. The proposal includes a 1,076 mile double cable network which:
(1) passes all the 263,000 households in the district of Columbia;
(2) provides for 30 one-way television channels initially with 34 additional channels available in the future for one-way and two-way services;
(3) calls for the local origination of television programmes in each of nine service areas to suit area needs and interests;
(4) provides two-way communications on an experimental basis starting during the first year of operation and extending throughout the district in the future.

The point-to-point links (a total of 148 miles) will handle two-way television, voice and data communications and link federal government and local facilities including hospitals, police station, colleges and universities, all the district's state schools and major business and commercial interests.

The television related services offered by the system include: television programmes of public interest, i.e. child care, health care, educational courses of all types, employment and housing, information on community meetings and locally originated television programmes.

The system will cope with technical innovations such as computer-aided instruction, safety alarms, automatic meter readings and selective power control services.

The system also provides the basic network for automatic traffic control and public safety surveillance.

The estimated cost of the network for one-way services is $30 million and about twice that for two-way facilities if provided by the tenth year of operation throughout the district. These costs would be met by subscriber fees, charges for renting channel time and by foundation and government fundings. The usual subscriber fee for a 12-channel one-way system is $5 per month; Mitre assume a basic subscriber fee for the initial single cable 30 channel one-way service of $3.50 per month, and if two-way services are included the system is expected to be economically viable at fees as low as $6 per month with 50% of the households connected.

Villes nouvelles - the two most advanced cable systems in France are at Cergy-Pontoise and Grenoble.

(i) Cergy-Pontoise

The new development at Cergy-Pontoise will be completed by 1990 and at the end of the century the population will be around 350,000.

Seven channels will eventually be made available, with the possibility of more being added at a later stage - some of these capable of being used for two-way facilities.

(ii) Grenoble

The present population of the new town of Grenoble-Echirolle is 15,000. By 1976 it will have reached 50,000. At present about 400 people are able to receive programmes via the cable network.

As well as the national channels four local channels will be used: an educational channel, an adult education channel, a "cultural" channel - possibly showing the archives of the ORTF, and a community channel. It is hoped that 40 hours of programming will be distributed on the four local channels. A staff of 21 will be employed full time by the local station.

The main trunk network, which has few branches, is made up of one or two coaxial cables laid in the ducts used for the ordinary telephone networks. Line-amplifiers are placed at approximately 300 metre intervals. The trunk route is joined to the feeder network of smaller diameter coaxial cables by impedance matching units. At the outlets a terminal unit prevents local interference being injected into the system.

At present most of the systems can carry a dozen channels. This number could be extended either by using the 88 to 174 MHz band with the addition of converters on the receivers, or by modifying the system. Two-way transmission will be possible. The return path signals will use the lowest frequency band, limited to 30 MHz. The signals are separated by filters at each of the line-amplifiers.

Waveguides - see page 31.

Table 1:   Summary of Domestic Cable Developments

Country	First cable system started	No. of homes connected (1972)	% of homes	Notes
UK	1951	2.2 M	13	Growth rate 12% p.a.
USA	1950	6.5 M	11	CATV systems may not be owned by TV stations 20% of cable stations originate local programmes (1973)
CANADA	1951	1.4 M	23	114 of 361 licensed cable systems are originating local programmes
IRELAND	1960 for Irish programmes only 1973 for British and foreign material	65,000	8	
FRANCE	1972 experimental services in a few towns			
ITALY	Independent cable companies ENDED OFFICIALLY 1973			Experiments in local broadcasting and community television, including some two-way, continue
NETHERLANDS		1.8 M	40	6 stations provide local programming
BELGIUM		450,000	14	11 programme channels include several from neighbouring countries
JAPAN	Two large-scale experiments currently underway - one at Tama New Town has 2,000 subscribers.			

Table 2: TELEPHONE NETWORKS: Bandwidth for various applications

Type of Channel	Bandwidth in Hertz	Data Speed Capability in Bits/Second	Possible Applications
Telegraph	120	50-75	TELEX. Telegraph machines of slow speed 7 characters/sec. Data collection. Remote control. Telemetry.
Telephone	3000-4000	 200 2400 4800	*Analogue:* (a) Voice-conference facilities. (b) X,Y plotter-electrowriter, written information transmitted instantaneously. (c) Facsimile-high definition, 90 lines/inch picture foolscap size in 5 minutes. (d) Slow-scan TV on equalized private lines. *Digital:* (a) Bothway data, time sharing etc. on switched or private lines. (b) Data communications on equalized private lines, tape or card, Cathode ray tube display, 'blackboard-by-wire'.
Broadcast quality	12,000	10,000	(a) Higher speed data (b) Slow-scan TV transmission (c) Higher speed facsimile
Group	48,000	48,000	Computer to computer operation (slow speed), line printer
Super-group	240,000	240,000	Newspaper facsimile. Full double page 5 minutes 1000 lines/inch
Master-group	1.2 M	1 - 10 M	(a) High speed store data (b) Videophone (c) Conference Television
Broadband	4.5 M 6.0 M 12.0 M	> 100 M	High speed data Entertainment quality TV

Table 3:   TELEPHONE NETWORKS: Summary of present and proposed developments

NETWORK	LOCAL	JUNCTION	TRUNK	INTERNATIONAL
Definition	Typically serves a small residential area from a local exchange	Typically links several local exchanges in an area (e.g. a city) to a main switching centre	These provide inter-city transmission and links between main switching centres	Inter-national and inter-continental links
Existing Systems	Consist at present almost entirely of pair-type cables which are used only 1% of available time, and which for speech use only 1% of available bandwidth	More than 70% consists of multi-core cable i.e. many circuits in parallel with same characteristics as local networks. There are some coaxial cable wide-band circuits but these are mainly used for data services on privately leased lines	In the USA, the UK and most European countries there is a very large commitment to analogue systems. Therefore VHF coaxial lines have been used with frequency division multiplexing to progressively increase the channel capacity of existing cable networks. The latest works at 60 MHz and has a capacity of 10,800 high quality telephone circuits over two coaxial pairs	These are provided by land and submarine cables and by both direct and satellite relay radio circuits
Bandwidths and Bit Rates	300 kHz or more available on equalized private lines but for speech 3 to 4 kHz is used and for music 12 kHz. If used with PCM a bit rate of 2 M bit/sec is possible which will provide 30 speech channels or any equivalent service	Currently the same as for local networks in most cases	Progressively grouping-up provides main routes with a capacity of 12 to 2,700 or more analogue audio channels. 1.5 M bit/sec 24-channel PCM systems are also in use in the USA, UK and Japan. These will be replaced by 30-channel systems conforming to the new international standard	Bandwiths available are determined both by the state-of-the-art and the economics of laying and operating submarine cables or launching and operating satellites
Future Plans and Possibilities	All longer-term developments will be based on the use of PCM techniques. One or more of the following methods will be used to connect individual subscribers: (a) a coaxial "ring" main (b) solid-state microwave radio links working in the 50-100 GHz range (c) fibre optic cables (with 10s to 100s of M bit/sec capabilities)	PCM systems will use coaxial or microwave links in 5-10 km hops working at 20 GHz. These would have a capacity of 200 to 500 M bit/sec which is equivalent to 3,600 telephone or 2 television circuits per channel	Several alternative very wide-band systems are under field trials in a number of countries e.g. (a) Coaxial cables 4.4 and 9mm diameter tubes capable of handling 120 M bit/sec or 500 M bit/sec. Equivalent to 1,800 telephone channels or 1 television channel or more per tube (b) Circular waveguides of 50mm diameter working at 30-100 GHz and providing 500 M bit/sec to 2 G bit/sec channel capacity. Would provide 300,000 telephone, 2,500 videophone or 200 two-way television circuits. (c) Microwave links working at 11 GHz in 30-50 km hops and providing a 120 M bit/sec channel.	More and better cables are still being laid and plans for very high capacity satellite circuits are well advanced.

[B. 8] COM.75.XVII/75 A